Survive The Coming Storm - Weaponize

When A Gun Isn't The Answer

By Ray Gano

Table of Contents

Part 5 Training To Defend

CHAPTER 11 - A Time To Train - Solo Training At Home - Recommended Videos

Part 1

The Situation

CHAPTER 1 - A Rise In Crime - Lawlessness In The Last Days

It was about 9:00 PM Sunday night.

Tracye got a post on her Facebook from a friend here in town.

A woman texted her fiancé the words "HELP ME"

The lady had been missing since Friday afternoon. She left work at the Scooter Store in New Braunfels, TX to pick up her son at school in San Antonio, but she never made it.

This morning she is found in a Laredo Hospital. That facility is almost 200 miles away.

What has happened is unknown at the moment. All we know is that her fiancé got texted those words.

This really concerned Tracye and me because at that time we lived in New Braunfels, TX which is a pretty small town.

Survive The Coming Storm – Weaponize – When A Gun Isn't The Answer – By Ray Gano

But that is not all. Here is another headline...

Man stabs woman outside New Braunfels Walmart

A woman was stabbed in an attempted purse snatching outside of a New Braunfels Walmart early Sunday.

The stabbing took place just before 11 a.m. in the parking lot of the Walmart off of I-35.

Police say the suspect tried to swipe a 64-year-old woman's purse. He also stabbed her several times before fleeing the scene.

The woman was air lifted to University Hospital and is in stable condition.

Source -
http://www.kens5.com/story/local/2015/05/06/10643299/

Here is one more...

Man Shot in an Attempted Brutal Kidnapping

NEW BRAUNFELS, Texas -- Glenn Shane Godden, 39, of Seguin, was killed by police after attempting to kidnap a woman.

According to police, it all started when a man called authorities and said his door had been kicked in..... and his 32-year-old daughter was missing.

When officers arrived, they saw a white van speeding away from the area, dragging a woman outside the car window, being held by her hair from the driver's side door.

According to police, Godden drove past one cruiser, but then rammed head-on into another police cruiser, landing on top of the hood.

The woman became pinned underneath both vehicles.

Source - http://www.ksat.com/news/26004360/detail.html

New Braunfels, TX has a population of around 45,000 people and yet Tracye and I were astounded at the violent crime that is taking place, especially in such a rather small quiet conservative town.

But what is worse is that crime of this nature is more and more becoming the norm no matter where one lives.

In fact, it is getting worse all over the nation.

The Index of Leading Cultural Indicators

In the early 1960s, the Census Bureau began publishing the Index of Leading Economic Indicators. These 11 measurements taken together represent the best means we now have of interpreting current business developments and predicting future economic trends.

From this idea The Index of Leading Cultural Indicators, a compilation of the Heritage Foundation and Empower America, attempts to bring a similar kind of data-based analysis to cultural issues. This report is a statistical portrait (from 1960 to the 1990s) of the moral, social and behavioral conditions of modern American society--matters that, in our time, often travel under the banner of ``values.''

It should not surprise you to learn that according to The Index of Leading Cultural Indicators, America has been deteriorating socially, morally and I believe spiritually over the past 30+ years.

Since 1960, the U.S. population has increased 41%; the total social spending by all levels of government has risen from $143.73 billion to the unimaginable $112 Trillion. This statistic represents an increase that people cannot even wrap their brains around.

Inflation-adjusted spending on welfare has increased by 630%+ and spending on education by 225%. But here is a shocker. Over this 30-year period, and again this report was published in the 1990s, there was an increase in violent crime by 560%, a 419% increase in illegitimate births; a quadrupling in divorce rates; a tripling of the percentage of children living in single-parent homes; more than a 200% increase in the teenage suicide rate; and a drop of almost 80 points in SAT scores.

That was over a course of 30 years. We are now 20+ years past that and without knowing the statistics, one can just tell that it has gotten even worse.

The fact that violent crimes are on the increase in sleepy little towns all over the US tells me that lawlessness is on the rise and getting worse by the day.

I mean should we expect it to be any other way when murder, violence, aggression are on TV 24/7/365?

I am going to go out on a limb here and say that based on the last 100 years one can clearly see that violence, lawlessness and the lack of "natural love" for one another has reached epidemic proportions.

It has gotten to the point that literally no place is safe... and it is getting worse.

Public schools resemble prison yard territories; kids are basically forced to join this social group or the next. On the streets gangs are rampant. In fact, children are not safe in their own homes anymore. They are beaten, maimed, raped, held as prisoners for sexual pleasure, then murdered because they become a burden and discarded as trash.

Remember the Caylee Anthony case?

Even though she was found not guilty, I honestly believe that it was the jury being lazy and not wanting to do their job properly. They opted for the desire to no longer be sequestered by the court instead of doing their proper job and issuing true justice.

Teenagers have lost all respect for authority. They have become cold, hard hearted, self-centered, selfish and violent.

"The increases in violence we're observing are among very young people and they are very dramatic," said Glenn Pierce, the director of Northeastern's Center for Applied Social Research.

This crime wave isn't confined to inner-city neighborhoods in large urban areas. Cities with populations of 25,000 saw a 40 percent increase in homicides - the same as cities 10 times their size.

Matthew 24:12 " And because iniquity shall abound, the love of many shall wax cold."

2 Timothy 3:1 "This know also, that in the last days perilous times shall come."

So should we be surprised at this getting even worse?

Couple what is going on today and add to the mix ISIS Terrorists that are now running operations here in the US

Enter ISIS, Global Terrorist Group and Hater of America

A few days ago, May 2015, two ISIS operatives tried to shoot up an event hosted by Pamela Geller in Garland, Texas. The event was about drawing the best picture of Mohamed, Islam's prophet.

This event was hosted as a free speech event to prove a number of things, primarily, that the first amendment in today's world does not apply equally to all. Muslim terrorists have more freedoms to express themselves than Christians do.

Draw a picture of Mohamed, and you are allowed to kill people. But dunk a crucifix of Christ in a jar of urine, and it is called art.

Thanks to Geller's foresight, she hired her own police security and the two ISIS terrorists were stopped before they could do their damage all in the name of Allah.

ISIS did not take long to issue a terrorist threat to Geller and all those who wish to be associated to her.

ISIS POSTS WARNING: "We Have 71 Trained Soldiers in 15 States" – ISIS NAMES 5 STATES AS TARGETS

The terrorist group says they will murder Pamela Geller and kill anyone who shields her.

The terrorists also say they have 71 fighters in 15 different states and they have signed up 23 individuals willing to die like the failed Sunday attack in Garland, Texas.

Bismillah Ar Rahman Ar Raheem

"The New Era"

To our brothers and sisters fighting for the Sake of Allah, we make dua for you and ask Allah to guide your bullets, terrify your enemies, and establish you in the Land. As our noble brother in the Philippines said in his bayah, "This is the Golden Era, everyone who believes... is running for Shaheed".

The attack by the Islamic State in America is only the beginning of our efforts to establish a wiliyah in the heart of our enemy. Our aim was the khanzeer Pamela Geller and to show her that we don't care what land she hides in or what sky shields her; we will send all our Lions to achieve her slaughter. This will heal the hearts of our brothers and disperse the ones behind her. To those who protect her: this will be your only warning of housing this woman and her circus show. Everyone who houses her events, gives her a platform to spill her filth are legitimate targets. We have been watching closely who was present at this event and the shooter of our brothers. We knew that the target was protected. Our intention was to show how easy we give our lives for the Sake of Allah.

We have 71 trained soldiers in 15 different states ready at our word to attack any target we desire. Out of the 71 trained soldiers 23 have signed up for missions like Sunday, We are increasing in number bithnillah. Of the 15 states, we will name 5- Virginia, Maryland, Illinois, California, and Michigan. The disbelievers who shot our brothers think that you killed someone untrained, nay, they gave you their bodies in plain view because we were watching.

The next six months will be interesting, To our Amir Al Mu'mineen make dua for us and continue your reign, May Allah ennoble your face.

May Allah send His peace and blessings upon our Prophet Muhummad and all those who follow until the last Day. —

Abu Ibrahim Al Ameriki

Source - https://justpaste.it/Anonymous90

The time has come where we realistically need to think about being ready to defend ourselves, those we love and care for and the innocent.

CHAPTER 2 - When They Come For Your Guns . . . You Will Turn Them Over

The second situation that we seriously need to consider is our guns being confiscated and our reliance upon the common bullet. I am one who believes that over the years we have become vulnerable because we have learned to depend solely on the gun and the bullet.

When we finally run out of ammo, what do we do then? This question is why this book is focusing more on non-gun defenses and more about keeping inconspicuous weapons around you at all times no matter where you are or what you are doing.

Now sure there are some blowhards out there who say they will die with their dead cold fingers around their guns, but in reality, that is all they are....blowhards; or they will be dead lying in a pool of their own blood.

We need to remember that we as Christians are called to a much higher calling. Matthew 28:19 does not tell us to die with our guns. It tells us that we are to go ye therefore and share the gospel with all the world. This is why it is called the Great Commission. Now Christ also said to arm ourselves. When we do so that we can protect the Gospel and protect ourselves. He said that if we do not have a sword, that we are to go out and buy one. Well, that is what I have done, and I train with my sword as well as other weapons. So no matter the environment I am able to arm myself with a weapon and defend myself and those I care about at a moment's notice.

In MANY cases, we will not be able to have a gun, even if we have a carry and conceal permit.

So we need to start training now so that we are NOT dependent upon the bullet and still be able to effectively defend ourselves or others.

In the end when the rubber meets the road, if our nation comes under martial law, people will get in line with everyone else and turn over their guns. This is a fact. Just look at what happened in Boston and New Orleans. The people complied. Even the blowhard "will die with my cold dead fingers on my gun" folks.

Survive The Coming Storm – Weaponize – When A Gun Isn't The Answer – By Ray Gano

In the end, when it comes to your shooting someone, then dying with 30 rounds going through your body, you will think again and turn over the gun.

To expand on this thought, here is an EXCELLENT article by Jim Karger who is an attorney and frequent contributor to several conservative news sources on the internet. He has written a lot on this topic and he understands human nature, the will to survive as well as the political and social arena we are now in today.

When They Come For Your Guns... You Will Turn Them Over

By Jim Karger

"When they come for my gun, they will have to pry it out of my cold, dead hands," is a common refrain I often hear from the Neo-Cons when there is a threat, credible or otherwise, that the US government is going to take their firearms.

And, when I hear this crazy talk, I agree with them openly. "You are right. They will pry your gun from your cold dead hands," which I often follow with the question, "And where will that leave you except face down in a pool of your own blood the middle of the street, just another dead fool resisting the State?"

This is not a question they are comfortable with, if only because the intent of their saber-rattling was to imply they would fight to keep their weapons, and win.

Nice fantasy. It's not happening.

If the federal government decides to disarm the public, and one of these (see photo below) rolls down your street after a not-so-subtle request that you kindly turn over your firearms and ammunition "for the common good," it will be nothing less than suicide by cop to do anything other than what you are told.

"Want to take this on?"

The militarization of US police forces is ongoing and escalating. Many cities and towns now own tanks, armed personnel carriers, even attack helicopters, and almost all are outfitted with military weapons not available to the general public.

Survive The Coming Storm – Weaponize – When A Gun Isn't The Answer – By Ray Gano

And, it is not just your hometown cops who are getting new boy-toys. The military itself is buying up weaponry not just for use in the current or next scheduled war, but to deal with the likes of you, citizens who don't seem to understand that the Bill of Rights has been overruled. That specifically includes, but is not limited to, the right to protest and engage in civil disobedience.

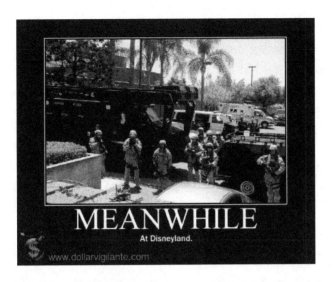

MEANWHILE
At Disneyland.
www.dollarvigilante.com

Also ignored (as if it didn't even exist) is the Posse Comitatus Act of 1878 which generally bars the military from law enforcement activities within the United States.

According to Public Intelligence:

"...for the last two years, the President's Budget Submissions for the Department of Defense have included purchases of a significant amount of combat equipment, including armored vehicles, helicopters and even artillery, under an obscure section of the FY2008 National Defense Authorization Act (NDAA) for the purposes of "homeland defense missions, domestic emergency responses, and providing military support to civil authorities." Items purchased under the section include combat vehicles, tanks, helicopters, artillery, mortar systems, missiles, small arms and communications equipment. Justifications for the budget items indicate that many of the purchases are part of routine resupply and maintenance, yet in each case the procurement is cited as being "necessary for use by the active and reserve components of the Armed Forces for homeland defense missions, domestic emergency responses, and providing military support to civil authorities" under section 1815 of the FY 2008 NDAA." (Emphasis supplied.)

And, they are not just arming cops and weekend warriors for domestic purposes. Active duty Marines are now being trained for law enforcement operations all over the world (of which the US remains a part) specifically to deal with civil uprisings, and the US government knows that civil uprisings are coming to a town near you just as soon as the fantasy of a healing economy is shattered, the US dollar fails, and unemployment goes to 30%+ in real numbers.

Survive The Coming Storm – Weaponize – When A Gun Isn't The Answer – By Ray Gano

And to you tough-talking Neo-Cons with your AR-15 rifles and a few thousand rounds of ammo, here is reality: they will take your guns, and no, all your Second Amendment bluster aside; you are not going to do anything about it. You are not going to take on a platoon of Marines with state of the art automatic weapons and the best body armor you cannot buy protected by armed personnel carriers and attack helicopters unless you choose to die that day — for nothing.

You will either be in the country or out, and if you are in, you will stay in; and you will comply.

That is your choice . . . for the moment.

About The Author

Jim Karger is a lawyer, and frequent contributor to The Dollar Vigilante, who has represented American businesses against incursions by government and labor unions for 30 years. In 2001, he left Dallas, TX and moved to San Miguel de Allende in the high desert of central Mexico. Here he sought and found a freer and simpler life for him and his wife, Kelly, and their 10 dogs. Karger's website is www.crediblyconnect.com.

CHAPTER 3 - Where Did We Go Wrong?

Over the years men of God have dropped the ball. They have allowed what I believe a "feminization" of the church to take place. More and more women "wore the pants" in churches than 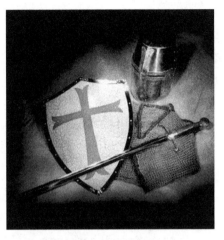 men. It is still that way today. More women attend church, are involved in church, and help direct church while basically men just hang at home to watch their football, baseball and basketball games on TV.

We as men of God have neglected our proper role and because of that abdication, society has taken on a more "feminized" viewpoint over what God's Word states.

Now I know that I may be upsetting some folks out there, but this is a fact and has been the fact for the past 125+ years.

Somewhere along the way, men lost their back bone.

The whole foundation of the family structure is based upon the man of the home doing the right thing, being a loving father and husband and disciplinarian, but also, to be the Christian warrior he is called to be. His role is to guide and protect his family as well as his community.

What does God's Word say?

> Psalms 144:1 Blessed be the LORD my strength, which teacheth my hands to war, and my fingers to fight.

> Jeremiah 48:10 Cursed be he that doeth the work of the LORD deceitfully, and cursed be he that keepeth back his sword from blood.

> Luke 22:36 Then said he unto them, But now, he that hath a purse, let him take it, and likewise his scrip: and he that hath no sword, let him sell his garment, and buy one.

And one that really hits home very hard...

> 1 Timothy 5:8 But if any provide not for his own, and especially for those of his own house,

he hath denied the faith, and is worse than an infidel.

Godly men's apathy has grown so bad that we are now suffering the consequences of our neglect.

Instead of standing and doing the right thing, we have gotten used to illicit sexual relationships, adolescent promiscuity, abortion, cheating, lying, stealing, prostitution, rape, divorce, and even murder. All of this has taken place because we as men of God have refused to stand in the gap and do what is right in light of God's Word.

We have become accustomed to financial mismanagement on both civil and personal levels. We have accepted political corruption. We have rejected personal and social responsibility and learned to blame anyone or anything else for our problems and failures. We have traded in our infinitely valued divine image for a nickel-plated pagan shrine erected in honor of self-interest, immorality, and social apathy.

What we need to do as men of God is to draw the line in the sand and say "no more."

Men of God need to learn to grow their back bone again and start being the men of God they are called to be.

We are at a stage in time where the wolves are becoming a serious menace to society. The only way to combat this threat is to once again become the "sheepdogs" that we were once many years ago.

We need to regain what we have lost. We need to learn how to be the proper leaders and not dictators in our families. We need to determine how to defend our families, and if called upon, to offer the ultimate sacrifice to protect them.

When walking in the parking lot with your family, let your body language state that you are the sheepdog and no one is going to accost those you have stewardship over.

Better yet, we need to obey Christ Himself and if we do not own a weapon, then we need to get one and do what we need to do so that we can protect our families.

Survive The Coming Storm – Weaponize – When A Gun Isn't The Answer – By Ray Gano

This does not mean go buy a gun and then stick it in the night stand drawer. We as Christian warriors need to train and become proficient so that when that evil day comes, we are able to stand and fight.(Eph6:13)

Our nation is going down the tubes; we are called as Christians to "occupy till He returns." That is our marching orders. We have to return to our duty until that time of our appointment with Him comes or till He calls His church home.

No matter what, we have a responsibility to ourselves and to our families.

Times ARE getting bad, and they will get even worse than what we have been seeing already. Scripture tells us that this will take place. God does not lie.

Therefore, until that time comes, we must be ready to stand for what is right and return to our heritage, to be the Christian Warrior God called us to be and stop neglecting the duties He has placed upon us.

Part 2

The Forgotten

Lessons

CHAPTER 4 - Turn The Other Cheek – The Cowards Favorite Verse

You do not know how many emails I get from ignorant cowards and so called pacifists who always quote "We are not supposed to fight, we are told to turn the other cheek."

This is primarily taken from Matthew.

> Matthew 5:39 But I say unto you, That ye resist not evil: but whosoever shall smite thee on thy right cheek, turn to him the other also.

It upsets me that so many who call themselves Christians today do not take the time to really study Scripture and look into the context from which a lot of popular ideas stem.

This is taken from Matthew 5 which is the beginning of the famous Sermon on the Mount, which goes all the way through to chapter 7.

In this portion Christ is talking about dealing with your enemies. The problem is that there are different types of enemies, enemy personal, enemy universal, enemy corporate. The pacifist lumps it all into one category, "enemy".

The problem is that what Christ is talking about here are personal enemies and not those who are corporate / universal.

When we read in context, we see that Christ is addressing social issues. How to deal with one another, being angry with one another, issues like adultery and divorce, making promises you cannot keep or making promises you should not promise to keep.

We then come to the famous turn the other cheek / love your enemy part.

> Matthew 5: 38-48 Ye have heard that it hath been said, An eye for an eye, and a tooth for a tooth:
>
> 39 but I say unto you, That ye resist not evil: but whosoever shall smite thee on thy right cheek, turn to him the other also.
>
> 40 And if any man will sue thee at the law, and take away thy coat, let him have thy cloke also.

41 And whosoever shall compel thee to go a mile, go with him twain.

42 Give to him that asketh thee, and from him that would borrow of thee turn not thou away.

43 Ye have heard that it hath been said, Thou shalt love thy neighbour, and hate thine enemy.

44 But I say unto you, Love your enemies, bless them that curse you, do good to them that hate you, and pray for them which despitefully use you, and persecute you;

45 that ye may be the children of your Father which is in heaven: for he maketh his sun to rise on the evil and on the good, and sendeth rain on the just and on the unjust.

46 For if ye love them which love you, what reward have ye? do not even the publicans the same?

47 And if ye salute your brethren only, what do ye more than others? do not even the publicans so?

48 Be ye therefore perfect, even as your Father which is in heaven is perfect.

In these verses, as well as in all of Chapter 5, Christ is dealing with personal social issues, not government or corporate issues.

Nowhere does it say that we cannot defend ourselves, not protect the innocent, and not protect our family.

Breaking Down "Turn The Other Cheek" - Which Hand?

> Matthew 5: 39 but I say unto you, That ye resist not evil: but whosoever shall smite thee on thy right cheek, turn to him the other also.

For the past 100 years we have stopped being a war like / fighting people. Because we are no longer fighters, we miss out on something that our forefathers understood plain as day.

Let's look at social norms.

First, the majority of the world is "right" handed. Why is that? I honestly believed that God created man to be right handed and to this day that still remains to be the norm. Only 15% of the world's population is left handed.

Throughout history and social norms the left hand is always the "unclean" hand. In the days before proper sanitary conditions, men and women used their left hand to deal with all their "nether regions" hygiene issues. This includes the monthly issues with which women have to contend.

SO... no one and I mean no one used the left hand for any sort of social interaction. To this day we still honor that idea.

Just as a quick test, reach your left hand to shake hands and watch the other person's eyes. You will see that you are "tripping them up" mentally. They will think a moment before offering the left hand, that is, if they even offer a hand at all.

In today's PC world where people don't ask "WHY" and do not want to "offend," most people will then shake with the left hand if given a few moments to think about it.

We can see that even Luke records the social norm when he references the Sermon on the Mount.

> Luke 6:29 And unto him that smiteth thee on the one cheek offer also the other; and him that taketh away thy cloke forbid not to take thy coat also.

When you read from the Authorized King James Bible, you will notice that the word "ONE" is italicized. It is italicized because he is referencing the "right" cheek or proper cheek. Luke is talking about the "right" side as opposed to the wrong side or second side.

The historical social norm is that the right side is always right / first, and the left side is always the wrong side, second or what is "left."

Do a study on right vs left in social norms. It is amazing to find out why we do what we do and this in and of itself shows that God is in fact our Creator and we did not just appear out of some primordial ooze. God put thought into us and ingrained these ideas into our DNA.

Now, with this little history lesson out of the way, let me ask you the following...

How does a right handed person "smite" or strike someone on the right cheek?

Think on this for a moment and hum the Jeopardy game show theme in your mind as you are thinking.

Ready?

The only way a right handed person could strike someone on the right cheek is use the back of the hand to slap them with what is commonly known as a backslap.

If you would "attack" someone and intend to do serious damage / fight a person, you would use a fist and strike the closest target, that being the left cheek.

But Christ is CLEARLY talking about the right cheek.

Because we are no longer a fighting warlike people, we miss the entire context of this message. Because of the consequent misinterpretation, we feminize the meaning. Since we have become so emasculated, we lose out on what Christ is telling us.

Context 1 – Christ is talking about social issues / treating one another.

Context 2 – one NEVER strikes another with a left hand. That is the unclean hand, and one just did not break that unwritten social rule no matter what.

Context 3 – In a fighting warlike society, if you backslap someone, it has always been seen as a form to bring shame / insult to the person who is being slapped.

To put it in modern terminology "Bi--h-slap" (think the proper term for a female dog)

To define this we read the following..

> Bi--h-slap
>
> "to hit someone's face (usually the cheek) with the back of one's hand. Typically performed when the person is being insubordinate and is used to assert one's authority, rather than to cause great harm. "

Christ is not talking about universal / corporate enemies, enemies at large or nation states that want to do us harm.

He is talking about that real jerk at work who always wants to up you by one, rub your nose in it when you make a mistake, the one who is always starting rumors about you, and the one who is most likely be the person who will take his or her keys and put a huge scratch down the side of your car.

That is the sort of enemy Christ is talking about here.

But because over the past 100 years we have gone from a fighting warlike people to a soft feminized PC culture,

"God is Love" sort of people, we have been missing this point.

Did Christ Turn The Other Cheek? HECK NO! The Lion of Judah Comes Out

How many of you know or remember the scene in the garden when Jesus was arrested? There is a lot going on here, but when you read all four accounts from the Gospels, we clearly see the "Lion of Judah" coming out In Christ and not some meek lamb that is often portrayed. In the garden Christ shows His street smarts as well as giving us a peek at the "Lion of Judah," even though He allowed Himself submission to being the "Lamb."

John gives an account with a lot of detail that the other gospels did not include. There is a lot there when we really take the time to read.

Please take the time to read the following. It is important, so please do not skim it, really read...

John 18: 2 – 11

2 And Judas also, which betrayed him, knew the place: for Jesus ofttimes resorted thither with his disciples.

3 Judas then, having received a band of men and officers from the chief priests and Pharisees, cometh thither with lanterns and torches and weapons.

4 Jesus therefore, knowing all things that should come upon him, went forth, and said unto them, Whom seek ye?

5 They answered him, Jesus of Nazareth. Jesus saith unto them, I am he. And Judas also, which betrayed him, stood with them.

6 As soon then as he had said unto them, I am he, they went backward, and fell to the ground.

7 Then asked he them again, Whom seek ye? And they said, Jesus of Nazareth.

8 Jesus answered, I have told you that I am he: if therefore ye seek me, let these go their way:

9 that the saying might be fulfilled, which he spake, Of them which thou gavest me have I lost none.

10 Then Simon Peter having a sword drew it, and smote the high priest's servant, and cut off his right ear. The servant's name was Malchus.

11 Then said Jesus unto Peter, Put up thy sword into the sheath: the cup which my Father hath given me, shall I not drink it?

Did you see the "lion" here?

First point - Judas betrays Christ with a kiss and then returns to the crowd of men. This in and of itself was seen as an insult. Luke even records Christ reaction to this insult...

Luke 22:48 But Jesus said unto him, Judas, betrayest thou the Son of man with a kiss?

In other words, "Judas, you know who I am (referring to the fact that He is God in the Flesh) and you betray me with a lowly kiss?"

He was basically calling Judas a coward and a weakling.

Second Point – Jesus recovers from the insult and boldly asks "Whom seek ye?" They answer back they are seeking Jesus of Nazareth.

Third Point – Many people miss the following: we witness The Lion's Roar, but John is the only one who records it...

> 5 They answered him, Jesus of Nazareth. Jesus saith unto them, I am he. And Judas also, which betrayed him, stood with them.
>
> 6 As soon then as he had said unto them, I am he, they went backward, and fell to the ground.

When Christ said " I AM HE, " He said it as a warrior and One with authority. Remember He was just insulted by the cowardly kiss that Judas gave him. He was letting the mass of people there know that He is The Lion of Judah, the Son of God, The Alpha and Omega.

He startled them so much that they all, including Judas, were stepping backwards and falling to the ground.

Now, to give you an idea of the large number of people there to arrest Christ, we read the following in Mark.

Mark 14:43 And immediately, while he yet spake, cometh Judas, one of the twelve, and with him a great multitude with swords and staves, from the chief priests and the scribes and the elders.

Here is a very good excerpt describing the "great multitude"…

I want you to understand exactly who this "band of men" and these "officers from the chief priests" were so you can see the full picture of what happened that night on the Mount of Olives. I believe you will be flabbergasted when you realize the gigantic numbers of armed men who came looking for Jesus that night!

The soldiers Judas brought with him to the Garden of Gethsemane were soldiers who served at the Tower of Antonia—a tower that had been built by the Hasmonean rulers. Later it was renamed the "Tower of Antonia" by King Herod in honor of one of his greatest patrons, Marc Antony (yes, the same Marc Antony who fell in love with the Egyptian queen Cleopatra!).

The Tower of Antonia was a massive edifice that

45

was built on a rock and rose seventy-five feet into the air. Its sides had been completely smoothed flat to make it difficult for enemies to scale its walls. Although it had many towers, the highest one was located on the southeast corner, giving the watchman an uninhibited view of the temple area as well as much of Jerusalem.

Inside this massive complex was a large inner courtyard for exercising the Roman cohort—comprised of 300 to 600 specially trained soldiers—who were stationed there. These troops were poised to act defensively in the event of an insurgency or riot. In fact, a staircase led from the tower into the temple; enabling the troops to enter the temple in a matter of minutes should a disturbance develop there.

One writer has noted that there was even a secret passageway from the tower to the inner court of the priests, making it possible for troops to reach even that holy, off-limits location.

John 18:3 records that there was "a band of

men" in the Garden that night. The Greek word for "a band of men" is spira.

This is the word that describes a military cohort—the group of 300 to 600 soldiers mentioned above. These extremely well-trained soldiers were equipped with the finest weaponry of the day.

Source - http://www.cfaith.com/index.php/article-display/31-articles/easter/15779-how-many-soldiers-does-it-take-to-arrest-one-man

This was a major event. Over 300 and more like 600 well-armed and well trained men came to take on Christ and his disciples.

Another fact that many people overlook is that the disciples were not any wimpy slouches themselves.

We read in Luke ...

Luke 22:49 When they which were about him saw what would follow, they said unto him, Lord, shall we smite with the sword?

These guys were itching for a fight. In fact, Peter jumps the gun and gets into it. He proceeds to cut off the ear of the high priest's personal servant.

Folks, these guys had fortitude (guts), and they were ready to start attacking at a drop of the hat.

Christ spoke with such warrior authority that the ENTIRE GROUP OF PEOPLE stepped back in shock causing ALL OF THEM to fall to the ground. Can you picture this?

Do you see the warrior / Lion of Judah I am painting for you here?

Do you understand that the disciples KNEW whom they served and KNEW whom they were with? Do you see and understand the bravado here that Christ and the disciples displayed?

Christ let himself be known to the crowd. His stating that "HERE I AM" clearly startled the mass of people, and I bet that they were seriously shaking in their boots too.

I say all this because often Christ, as well as the disciples, is made out to be a bunch of hippy dippy sissy men.

NO.. they were not. They were hard core take- it- to- the mat men of God.

This is our example; all of us need to learn to boldly stand again, just as Christ and the disciples did when they were confronted with "their enemy."

Now it is from the following portion that the cowardly pacifists, the wimpy men get another one of their famous out of context ideas.

"Live By The Sword, Die By The Sword."

> Mark 14: 46 And they laid their hands on him, and took him.
>
> 47 And one of them that stood by drew a sword, and smote a servant of the high priest, and cut off his ear.
>
> 48 And Jesus answered and said unto them, Are ye come out, as against a thief, with swords and with staves to take me?

49 I was daily with you in the temple teaching, and ye took me not: but the scriptures must be fulfilled.

We can see the warrior again exert his authority, challenging the mass of people. In fact, does Christ turn the other cheek?

NO!

He accuses them and holds them accountable.

" HEY... you had the chance during the day to come get Me, but you did not have the courage. But now you come in the dark with your swords and staffs being all macho? Some "men" you are! " You want me? HERE AM I !!"

So here is Jesus with 11 rag tag men, all of them armed and ready to fight. Then Christ shows how He is the compassionate Servant Warrior. He heals the ear of servant and then reminds them that the Scriptures must be fulfilled.

I have to say that if the Scriptures did not have to be fulfilled, maybe they might have gone at it right then...right there. This was a very tense situation.

But we learn another insight, even though the disciples KNEW with whom they were joining in the fight. Christ also shows wisdom in saying " those who fight by the sword will die by the sword."

In other words, when you read it in proper context, Christ was telling the disciples that they were greatly outnumbered and that now was not the day for all of them to die. He was proud of them, but He pointed out that the Scriptures must be fulfilled and to do that, He had to submit to God's Will and allow Himself to be taken.

But That Is Not All… Still No Turning the Other Cheek

So here is the situation. Jesus submitted and allowed the High Priest and the entire rabble to take him away. Then things get interesting again.

> John 18:19 The high priest then asked Jesus of his disciples, and of his doctrine.
>
> 20 Jesus answered him, I spake openly to the world; I ever taught in the synagogue, and in the temple, whither the Jews always resort; and in secret have I said nothing.

21 Why askest thou me? ask them which heard me, what I have said unto them: behold, they know what I said.

22 And when he had thus spoken, one of the officers which stood by struck Jesus with the palm of his hand, saying, Answerest thou the high priest so?

23 Jesus answered him, If I have spoken evil, bear witness of the evil: but if well, why smitest thou me?

24 Now Annas had sent him bound unto Caiaphas the high priest.

Christ is taken captive and presented to the High Priests' HQ for questioning. Look at the words here in John 18. I am sorry, but this does not sound like a person who is a wimpy, limp wristed sissy man like He is portrayed today.

Survive The Coming Storm – Weaponize – When A Gun Isn't The Answer – By Ray Gano

Annas asked him about all the doctrine, the disciples and what he taught, and Jesus got right back at him in Annas' face and asked him "Why are you asking me?" (Christ knew that Annas already knew the answer) Why don't you ask those who heard me? They know what I said!"

That is when one of Annas' officers then struck Jesus with the palm of his hand. Remember the social norms. Here the officer used his right hand but did not strike his right side. He stuck Christ's left cheek, the closest target.

DID JESUS TURN THE OTHER CHEEK HERE?

NO!

What did Jesus do?

He looked the guy in the eye, you know that look that shoot knives, and said " HEY... If I said something wrong, then tell me so I can make amends, otherwise why are you back-slapping me Bub ?"

We do not see Christ turning the other cheek here. In fact, He spoke up and asked why he was being insulted in such a manner when He did not do anything wrong. A slap is an insult; a fist is an attack.

Folks, since we have become a non fighting war like people, we have gotten soft. More than that we have lost perspective and social context in regards to our Lord and Savior.

He was not a long haired wimpy, spineless man. He was and is the Son of God. and He did not take garbage from people. When He saw wrong, He dealt with it; but He also showed us how to be a true Servant Warrior.

We need to get this feminized, emasculated idea of Christ out of our minds. We need to start realizing Who it is we serve. HE is the Lion of Judah. He is compassionate but strong. He is loving, but will not tolerate the bozos of the world who sneak in at dark to attack. He stands up for what is just, right and true.

I challenge you to start reading the gospels again and start looking for the Warrior Lion of Judah Who is our Lord. Forget about this weak, blue eyed hippy portrayal that so many people attribute Him.

Christ was The Warrior King, is The Warrior King and when all is said and done, will be The Warrior King when The Day of The Lord takes place.

This is the Man we need to emulate, not the Man those cowardly, retiring men and feminist pacifists have forced down our throats.

If anything, Christ shows us that we need to stand our ground, and these so called enemies are nothing. We serve the King of Kings. If they slap us in the face, we ask them if they want the other cheek to slap. If they want our coat, take it off and throw it in their face and ask them if they want your shirt as well.

We need to start standing like true men and women of God. We are a people who have a back bone, we know Who it is we serve. We serve The Warrior King - King Jesus - The Lion of Judah!

> Ephesians 6:13 Wherefore take unto you the whole armor of God, that ye may be able to withstand in the evil day, and having done all, to stand.

CHAPTER 5 - Live By The Sword Die By The Sword – The Coward's Second Favorite Verse

In the last chapter we focused on "Turn The Other Cheek ."

I want to focus next with the coward's second favorite verse, "Live by the sword, die by the sword."

> Matthew 26:52 Then said Jesus unto him, Put up again thy sword into his place: for all they that take the sword shall perish with the sword.

What people fail to do is remain in context. They cherry pick the verses to prop up their false ideas.

When we take the time to read in context, we find out that what is taking place here was Christ was being betrayed by the coward Judas. I call him coward because he sold out our Lord for 30 pieces of silver.

Judas brought with him about 300 and more like 600+ men to capture Christ.

Think about that for a second.

That is a lot of men to bring carrying staffs and swords. Because of the large number of this mob, it is clear that they (the mob) were afraid of Christ and his disciples.

Jesus & The Disciples Were No Sissy Boys

So many people make our Lord and Savior out to be some emasculated sissy boy. Folks, Our Lord was a carpenter. Think about the skills needed. If he wanted to build something, He did not run down to the local home depot and purchase the lumber and supplies. He took his ax and went to the forest and cut the tree down. He then hauled it back to his shop and shaped that log into workable lumber. Once workable, he then created the item that was needed or used the timber in home construction.

Our Lord was buffed, toned and had great strength to perform his skill. He wasn't the 110 pound weakling that so many people like to portray Him.

Look at the disciples for a second. Most of these guys were fishermen. Look at how tough fishermen are, hauling nets, moving gear, pulling in the fish. That puts muscle on you doing this day in and day out.

We learn that Matthew was tax collector. That means he knew how to get in people's faces and get the taxes. He probably was not afraid to back people down.

Looking at Luke, who was not a disciple but it is believed he followed Jesus and the 12. He was one of the 72 men that Christ first sent out. Luke was a doctor, and it is factual that he was in charge of treating all the men in the group; that is, if Jesus did not take of the minor wounds, scrapes and other injuries himself.

I look back in my days in the military when I served with special ops. We worked in 12 man teams, and one of those men was always a medic. Not only did he carry the standard battle load that we all carried (lots of bullets, grenades, belts of ammo for the machine gun, etc.), but also, he carried the groups' medical gear which was a separate backpack in and of itself that weighed about 30+ lbs. We humped going from objective to objective conducting raid, ambushes, assaults, recons. SO when we were able to take a break and sit for a moment, our medic did not have that luxury. He instantly went into action checking feet for blisters, any minor wounds, cuts, abrasions to prevent infection. Checked folks to make sure they were drinking enough water to prevent heat stroke. When he was done checking, he only got something like 15   20 minutes break on his own before we were moving out again to the next objective.

All of us looked up to our medic because this guy, as with many Spec Ops medics, was hard core.

This is why I believe that Doctor Luke was also pretty hardcore in that he probably carried all his own medical gear, supplies so that he could treat his own team. He could not run down to the local Walgreens pharmacy and get his supplies. Even if he did not use it, he was still carrying all the gear and making sure people were ok. He is a doctor; He can't help but care.

When this mob of 300 to 600 + men showed up, the disciples were ready to throw down. We know this because it is recorded …

> Luke 22:49 When they which were about him saw what would follow, they said unto him, Lord, shall we smite with the sword?

These guys were itching for a fight. In fact, Peter jumps the gun and gets into it with the high priest's servant and proceeds to cut off the guy's ear.

Folks, the disciples had fortitude (guts), and they were ready to start attacking at a drop of the hat.

But Christ realized that they were HIGHLY outnumbered. Could he have done something about it? Yes he could have, but He also submitted to God and the Scriptures and did not want anyone hurt or killed.

It is at this time that he states the following...

> Matthew 26:52 Then said Jesus unto him, Put up again thy sword into his place: for all they that take the sword shall perish with the sword.

This is the proper context of this verse.

It is Not this wimpy attitude that all these pacifist, limp wristed, sissy men have today saying that we should not defend ourselves, our wives, our children, our property, our neighborhoods.

Christk **COMMANDED** Us To Weaponize Ourselves

> Luke 22:36 Then said he unto them, But now, he that hath a purse, let him take it, and likewise his scrip: and he that hath no sword, let him sell his garment, and buy one

This is a portion of Scripture that a lot of people do not know about, especially the spineless pacifists. Christ COMMANDED us to weaponize ourselves, not only for our protection, but also for the sake of the Gospel.

> Luke 22:35-38 And he said unto them, When I sent you without purse, and scrip, and shoes, lacked ye any thing? And they said, Nothing.

36 Then said he unto them, But now, he that hath a purse, let him take it, and likewise his scrip: and he that hath no sword, let him sell his garment, and buy one.

37 For I say unto you, that this that is written must yet be accomplished in me, And he was reckoned among the transgressors: for the things concerning me have an end.

38 And they said, Lord, behold, here are two swords. And he said unto them, It is enough.

Again, go back to the context. Here we are at the last supper, and Christ is talking to the disciples. He is reminding them of the time that He told them to go out and spread the news about the Kingdom of God. He told them NOT to take anything because He wanted them to have faith in Him.

Now that they do have faith in Him and know who He is, The Son of God, Christ knows that they will stand to the very end to defend the Gospel. They will take the good news to the world.

This is why he tells us all to sell what we have so that we can "buy a sword, " enabling us to continue to share the Gospel in a horribly dark world.

IF you are a Christian and you do NOT have the means to protect yourself and protect the Gospel, then you are not following what Christ told you..us ...to do.

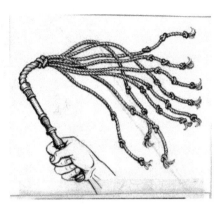

If you have not, you are being disobedient.

If you are balking at that, you are in rebellion.

Both of these behaviors are not pleasing to the Lord, and you will be held accountable for your disobedience. I pray that nothing happens to you, your family, or those innocent persons whom you can help or the Gospel in your area.

The sword at that time was the primary weapon of the day. If Christ said that today, odds are that he would say to go buy yourself a gun so that you can protect yourself and protect the sharing of the Gospel.

Jesus Weaponized Himself

John 2:12-16 After this he went down to Capernaum, he, and his mother, and his brethren, and his disciples: and they continued  there not many days.

13 And the Jews' Passover was at hand, and Jesus went up to Jerusalem,

14 and found in the temple those that sold oxen and sheep and doves, and the changers of money sitting:

15 and when he had made a scourge of small cords, he drove them all out of the temple, and the sheep, and the oxen; and poured out the changers' money, and overthrew the tables;

16 and said unto them that sold doves, Take these things hence; make not my Father's house an house of merchandise.

Did you see where he made a weapon and then used it to defend God's House?

He made a "scourge of small cords." In other words Christ made a cat of nine tails – a dangerous whip.

Christ was enraged. HE BECAME ANGRY that His Father's House was turned into a den of thieves, buying, selling, changing money from roman to temple money, and all these things being done at a very nice profit.

He created a weapon and cleansed the temple.

So once again the idea of some sissy man so many have painted Christ out to be is in fact a feminized fairytale.

Christ taught to defend what is right.

He taught that it is right to weaponize ourselves, protect ourselves and protect the means to share the Gospel.

Our Lord and Savior is the Lion of Judah. We need to obey Him.

We need to get back to being obedient to God's Word.

FOLKS... wake up and smell the coffee. One Christian dies - is martyred – every 11 minute, and this number is growing.

We as Christians need to grow a backbone and start realizing that we are in serious danger from many directions but most of all from Islam.

Islam makes it very clear that they are to kill and behead the Jew and the Christian. This is written in their own book, not once either, but multiple times. Their book calls for the death of the infidel. If you are not a believer and sold out to Islam 100%, you are the infidel. You are to be given the chance to convert, be enslaved and live under Sharia law (dhimmitude) or killed.

We as Christians cannot convert nor can we agree to live under Sharia law. So we either fight or defend ourselves, or we go to the chopping block.

NOTE... Muslims are not being nice and using the fabled guillotine that you hear all the rumors about on the internet. No, they are using butcher knives, AK-47 bayonets, and just about any other blade they can get their hands on.

This is a gruesome death and you cognizant of what is taking place as it is happening. It finally stops when your spinal cord is severed or your body goes into shock. In both cases you lose consciousness and finally die.

I have shared this video before, it is pretty gruesome; but this is the sort of brutality that will take place here.

WARNING – This video is VERY graphic, but I think people need to understand the brutality we are going to have to deal with.

WATCH   NOW   >>
http://www.liveleak.com/view?i=6b8_1398446167

People need to wake up and realize that this is what is coming. We have had a beheading in the US already. Beheadings are also taking place in England and in many other places in the world. There have been other Muslims attempting to behead others in lone ranger attacks all over the western world.

This is just the beginning of the war; it is going to get worse.

Ecclesiastes 3 tells us that there IS a time for hate, a time for war, a time to fight and a time to kill.

I REFUSE to bow to Islam and its demonic minions.

I WILL fight with my last breath to defend my wife, my family, the innocent and the Gospel.

I take my example from Christ as well as my command for me to weaponize myself.

Folks, no matter what, there is no talking to the followers of Islam. There is no reasoning, no compromises, no getting along.

Their book clearly states that we are to die... period.

True warriors fight not because they hate what is in front of them. They fight because they love what is behind them.

> 1 Timothy 5:8 But if any provide not for his own, and specially for those of his own house, he hath denied the faith, and is worse than an infidel.

> Nehemiah 4:14 And I looked, and rose up, and said unto the nobles, and to the rulers, and to the rest of the people, Be not ye afraid of them: remember the Lord, which is great and terrible, and fight for your brethren, your sons, and your daughters, your wives, and your houses.

> Joshua 24:15 And if it seem evil unto you to serve the LORD, choose you this day whom ye will serve; whether the gods which your fathers served that were on the other side of the flood, or the gods of the Amorites, in whose land ye dwell: but as for me and my house, we will serve the LORD.

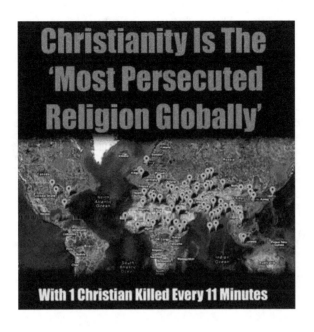

With 1 Christian Killed Every 11 Minutes

Survive The Coming Storm – Weaponize – When A Gun Isn't The
Answer – By Ray Gano

Part 3

Time To Defend

CHAPTER 6 - Our Current Situation It's Time To Stand And Defend

Tracye and I have been talking that there is a need for the common person to start thinking about protecting themselves.

Do you know that if you brought a knife to a gun fight, you would most likely win?

This is called The Tueller Drill.

Sergeant Dennis Tueller, of the Salt Lake City, Utah Police Department wondered how quickly an attacker with a knife could cover 21 feet (6.4 m), so he timed volunteers as they raced to stab the target. He determined that it could be done in 1.5 seconds. These results were first published as an article in SWAT magazine in 1983 and in a police training video by the same title, "How Close is Too Close?"?"

That means that a person that is approximately 21 feet from you or less, they will be able to attack you before you are able to draw a gun.

Watch this following police training video showing that the person with the knife has the advantage over the person with the gun.

WATCH NOW >>> https://youtu.be/J_KJ1R2PCMM

That means that one of your most important skills that you have is your situation awareness. In other words, knowing what is going on around you at all times.

In the Army we used to say, "Stay alert – Stay alive"

That is what is needed today.

Fight For Them – They Are Your Home

Tracye and I really do not watch regular TV anymore. We will turn on Fox News, but that is about it. What we do watch is a lot of Netflix so that we can control what shows we watch and stay away from a lot of the filth that is on TV.

Last night we were watching Longmire, it is a modern western TV show, kind of like Gunsmoke for today.

In the show there was a scene with Henry Standing Bear (played by Lou Diamond Philips) where he is quoting from a supposed Cheyenne legend... "What Did The First Warrior Say To The Great Spirit"

I am not sure of its authenticity, but it touched a chord with me and reminded me of what it means to live the Servant Warrior life.

We are to honor God always and protect the innocent, and the ones we love.

Thought I'd share it with you all.

> "The First Warrior looked out on the land and
> his Home.
> He saw the hills
> And the stars
> And he was happy.
> For giving him his home, the first warrior told
> the Great Spirit
> That he would fight and win many battles in His
> honor.

But the Great Spirit said, "No, do not fight for me.
Fight for your tribe,
Fight for the family born to you,
Fight for the brothers you find.
"Fight for them," the Great Spirit said, "for they are your Home."

This is the attitude that all of us must acquire. We need to be our brother's keeper again and care. We need to start being situationally aware so that we can cover each other's back.

"According to American Police Beat, the average response time for an emergency call is 10 minutes. Atlanta has the worst response time with 11 to 12 minutes and Nashville comes in at a lightning speed of 9 minutes."

The Department of Justice, with their statistical prowess, reports that the best response time is 4 minutes and the worst over 1 hour.

Source - http://www.self-defense-mind-body-spirit.com/average-police-response-time.html

A lot can happen in 10 minutes. This is why I say that we must start taking responsibility for our lives and for the lives of those we care about around us.

US Suffers Its First Beheading

Woman Beheaded In Oklahoma By Muslim Convert

A fired employee who had been trying to convert co-workers to Islam stabbed two female colleagues - beheading one of them - before an off-duty officer shot him, police have said.

After beheading Colleen Hufford, 54, and stabbing Traci Johnson, 43, multiple times, Nolen was shot by off-duty officer Mark Vaughan, who was working at the business.

During Thursday's attack, Nolen beheaded Colleen Hufford, 54, with the same kind of knife used in the plant, Lewis said.

Lewis said Nolen also stabbed Traci Johnson, 43, a number of times before company CEO Mark Vaughan, a reserve sheriff's deputy, shot him.

Source - http://nation.foxnews.com/2014/09/26/women-beheaded-oklahoma-muslim-convert

This is the first incident of beheading by a devout Muslim here in the US, well at least that we know of.

It isn't going to be the last either.

People need to wake up. Jihad is now on our shores. It has been here for some time now; we just had our heads in the sand about it.

Well, we need to pull our heads out of the sand.

But we need to do more than just that. We need to be ready to defend and fight these demons in the flesh.

Like it or not, we are witnessing the beginnings of a religious war.

We no longer have that choice to stay out of this fight. To do nothing allows evil to prevail.

This event is a great example of why we need to regain our resolve and learn to fight again.

We have been the sheep for too long. Now the wolves are beginning the slaughter.

It is time for the Servant Warrior to stand up and start caring for those whom he or she loves. It is time to stop being the sheep and start being the sheepdog.

The true warrior fights not because he hates what is in front of him. He fights because he loves what is behind him.

This event took place at a meat packing plant. The Muslim killer used one of the knives just like the meat packing plant used to cut the meat.

We need to start weaponizing ourselves so that we are always ready to protect and defend if the situation arises.

Part 4

The Tools To

Defend

CHAPTER 7 – Tools To Defend The Home

I am one who believes that one should try to make their home as invasion proof as possible. This is why I am big on early warning and entry provision.

Where we live I have implemented several security systems.

First, I have the Voice Alert System-6 Home/driveway Alarm system. I learned about this from a friend of mine when I heard his announcing that someone was at the side of the house, and then it announced that someone was by the tool shed. Come to find out it was just his dog, and he forgot to turn set the alarm to daytime.

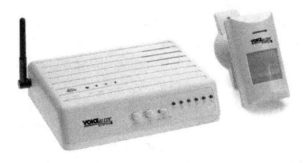

After researching extensively on pricing and features, I had to agree that this was a great system to give us early warning.

Here is what it says about the system on Amazon.

Would you like to be alerted when...

- Cars are coming up the driveway
- Children go inside your tool shed
- Intruders approach the front or backyard
- Someone enters your garage
- Visitors are walking to the front door
- Your parked boat or motor home has been boarded
- Kids or pets are trampling your flowers .

If you answered yes to the above, then you need the Voice Alert System-6.

System-6 allows a maximum of six user recorded messages. Each message is specific to one zone. For instance, zone one could be for a driveway alarm - "Car coming up the driveway" while zone two could be for a sensor monitoring the back yard- "Alert! Child by the pool!" Perhaps a third sensor guards a side entrance against intruders. However, when this PIR detects movement, the base unit plays

"Intruder on patio" and triggers a floodlight using one of four relays included on the base unit.

System-6 can monitor all three zones simultaneously and still have three additional zones available when needed. Users can alter their messages and place the wireless sensors wherever they wish.

Voice Alert System-6 sets up in minutes and can be completely customized to fit their individual needs.

The wireless PIRs feature: all weather protection, adjustable mounting and sensitivity, and can send a signal 300 feet through walls and up to 1000 feet in open space.

This is not some cheap system either. Each senor costs about $50.00 per, and they are weather proof. I have multiple sensors all over our perimeter giving us early warning of anyone entering our yard. They are the best out there for the dollar when it comes to home security systems that you can install yourself.

Another item that I totally recommend is a product called the Buddy Door Jammer.

The Buddy Door Jammer is another resource. I own one of these myself, and I can attest to the strength that this security stick has. Using this properly will make your door almost impenetrable. The person/s will have to destroy your door to get in.

Here is good video review of the Buddy Door Jammer.

WATCH NOW >>> https://youtu.be/gGVNawkgibw

This is an expensive door jammer, but it is worth it. It will definitely slow down anyone who is trying to forcibly gain access to your home.

Another good door lock is the FLIP LOCK. These are pretty inexpensive, and you can get them at most hardware stores. Putting multiple locks on one door will also slow down a home invader. Combine both the Buddy Bar and the Flip locks, and you will have a pretty secure door that intruders will have to destroy before they are able to get in.

If you have large windows or glass doors, you need to look into 8 Mil Window film.

The 8 Mil Window Film is a GREAT product and could possibly save your life. I have done studies on it that show if you apply it to both sides of the window, it will prevent bricks, large rocks and in some cases even a single shotgun blast using bird shot or small game shot and even a 22 bullet.

Now I would not stand in front of the window to test it, but in some of the case studies I have seen, this stuff is worth the money. People will not come in by breaking your window. That is a guarantee. They will have to pull the entire window glass out of the frame before they are able to gain access to the home.

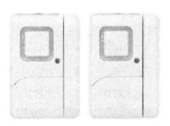

Another item that I have around our home is the GE Personal Alarm System.

I learned about these several years ago by a fellow prepper buddy, "Southern Prepper 1" and have put many of these in place in windows, doors, and also created trip wires like you can see in this video from Southern Prepper 1

WATCH NOW >>> Early Warning Combat Multipliers - https://youtu.be/QMB4m41IXfA

What happens if a person gains access? Again the focus is defense without a gun. So what can you do to defend yourself against would be invaders?

I am a huge fan of Cold Steel Inferno. This is a pepper spray that is foam, but once it is on the person, it melts and is very difficult to wash off. This stuff is bad to the bone and because it is a foam, you do not have to worry about a breeze blowing liquid pepper spray mist back in your own face. This is one of the problems with most liquid pepper sprays. Cold Steel has that flaw covered.

I highly recommend that people keep a good flashlight by their bed in case of an emergency. Why not have a good weapon and light at the same time?

My go to flashlight and stun gun is the Zap Million Volt Flashlight. This is actually a rechargeable million volt stun gun, and it is wicked. But you know what? It has a pretty good flashlight on it as well. This is perfect for the

Survive The Coming Storm – Weaponize – When A Gun Isn't The Answer – By Ray Gano

office, for on walks, keeping in your purse or backpack, use it to walk to your car, there are a lot of uses for it. I have had mine for over 2 years, and it still holds a great charge. Push the button and it is like lightning going off. It is very easy to operate and even in a panic one could use it with ease.

The Zap Flashlight is also hefty enough that if you wanted to use it as an impact weapon, well it would do the job. It has some weight to it, and it is a tad bulky. That is good when you need to slam this into someone and then let them have a million volts. You get this on any bad guy and push the button, they will drop. THEN.... while you have them down, zap them again for a good 10 seconds to make sure they are not getting back up for several long minutes. This is a good time to pull out the Cold Steel Pepper Spray and spray the bad guy in the face for a double whammy. They will not be getting up, and good chances are that you will be the family hero for taking out the bad guy.

Man uses katana to stop home invasion. This is the gory aftermath

Let's face it, we all know someone who has a few samurai swords. Whether they're there to prevent a home invasion, or an attack by zombies after the SHTF has occurred, everyone has a reason for owning swords.

Well, in this case, the swords came to a very good use and helped to defend a man's family from home invaders. This is the gory aftermath. The home invaders were stopped immediately upon entry into the man's home. They bailed to their getaway car but did not make it very far due to massive blood loss. They were found by police shortly after driving away, both unconscious due to blood loss.

CLICK HERE TO SEE WHAT A KATANA CAN DO TO FOUR ARMED HOME INVADERS WARNING – THIS IS VERY GRAPHIC AND BLOODY

http://knowledgeglue.com/man-uses-katana-stop-home-invasion-gory-aftermath-nsfw/

This is one of the reasons that I am a huge fan of the Katana, aka Samurai sword. It is a very easy weapon to use and if you can swing a golf club or baseball bat, you can do a lot of damage to a home invader.

The Katana is a weapon that a common person can quickly learn to use and actually use effectively if they get out in the back yard and practice cutting bottles and other objects.

I am very partial to the Musashi Company and their excellent swords. Not only are they great quality, but they are priced right too. For about $100 you can have a sword that is truly battle ready and a beautiful piece of art.

Here is the description from Amazon...

Part of a new 1060 high carbon series from Musashi. With the result being well within that goal, this blade is nothing short of an excellent value. Handmade, the blade hamon is formed by the clay temper  process during production. The blade is differentially hardened and comes extremely sharp. Like the more expensive models, this blade can even be bent 45 degrees and returned to the straight and true form. This sword is well balanced and the tight handle wrap feels great.

Materials and Way of Forge:

- Traditional hand forge Muku-kitae method.
- 1060 High Carbon Steel with clay temper process.
- 55 HRC blade hardness. Hamon and hardness created with temper process.
- Real hamon, not wire brushed or printed.
- Real ray skin wrapped grip with black cotton cord wrap.
- Extremely sharp hand honed edge.
- Steel tsuba, fuchi, and kashira; Brass habaki.
- Can be disassembled for care or display. Dual bamboo mekugi (peg), hardwood handle.
- Hardwood scabbard with high quality piano paint finish.
- 39 3/4 in. overall, 27 1/2 in. blade, 10 3/4 in. handle.
- Includes black cotton sword storage/carry bag.

Here is a video review of my Musashi 1060 Clay DH hardened katana.

Musashi 1060 Differentially Hardened Katana - Review - https://youtu.be/qEpHfAQKnq8

Here is my video of me cutting banana trees with my Musashi Katana.

Musashi 1060 DH Katana First Cuts Vs. A Banana Tree - https://youtu.be/TOUq2sMH_0M

There are many other things that you can do to help harden your home defenses, but the key is to make the bad guy ask himself "do I really want to go into this guy's home?"

Home intruders do not want a fight. They want to get in, get stuff and get out. The more things you have in place to deter the bad guy, the better.

Here are links to the products that I have talked about as well as some other items that I like, but I do not own as I have not tried them as of yet.

Items I Recommended In This Chapter

Voice Alert Alarm System - http://tinyurl.com/PZ-Voice-Alert-Alarm-System

Buddy Bar Door Jammer - http://tinyurl.com/PZ-BUDDY-BAR

Flip Action Door Lock - http://tinyurl.com/PZ-Flip-Door-Lock

8 Mil Security Window Film - http://tinyurl.com/PZ-Security-Window-Film

GE Personal Window / Door Alarm - http://tinyurl.com/PZ-GE-Personal-Alarm

Cold Steel Inferno 2.5 oz / 70 grams - http://tinyurl.com/PZ-Cold-Steel-Inferno-70grams

Cold Steel Inferno 1.3 oz / 37 grams - http://tinyurl.com/PZ-Cold-Steel-Inferno-37grams

Zap Million Volt Flashlight - http://tinyurl.com/PZ-Zap-Million-Volt-Flashlight

Musashi - 1060 Carbon Steel - Clay Tempered Samurai Sword *SHARP* - http://tinyurl.com/PZ-Musashi-Clay-Temprd-Katana

My Musashi DH 1060 sword - http://tinyurl.com/Musashi-1060-DH-Katana

Sabre Home Defense Pepper Spray - http://tinyurl.com/PZ-Home-Defense-Pepper-Spray

Doberman Ultraslim Window Alarm - http://tinyurl.com/PZ-Ultraslim-Window-Alarm

Door Stop Alarm - http://tinyurl.com/PZ-Doorstop-Alarm

Survive The Coming Storm – Weaponize – When A Gun Isn't The Answer – By Ray Gano

Window and Door Alarm - http://tinyurl.com/PZ-Window-Door-Alarm

Survive The Coming Storm – Weaponize – When A Gun Isn't The Answer – By Ray Gano

CHAPTER 8 – Tools To Defend The Work Place

Many offices and workplaces do not allow firearms on the premises due to liability.

Do not let that stop you. Weaponize your work area with common everyday items.

Example, this event took place in a meat packing plant. That means people are used to seeing knives everywhere. Learn to use the weapons around you. There were knives in that work environment. Learn to use the knife as a weapon.

What you want to do is look around in your work environment and see what you could use as a weapon or what common item could you weaponize.

Weaponize Your Workplace

If you are under 65, odds are that you spend a good amount of your time at your place of employment.

If you are like most people, you work in a cubical; so why not weaponize your area?

How many of you drink tea or coffee at the office? Do you have your own mug? I know that I did, and I was never without it the entire time I was at the office. Where ever I was, my mug was with me.

So why not "weaponize" and replace that Garfield The Cat coffee mug with a stainless steel coffee mug? People are used to seeing you with a coffee mug. They will not think twice seeing you with a weaponized stainless steel coffee mug. In fact, most of your co-workers will not even realize it is a weapon. They will just think that your spouse got you a cool present and that will be the last of it. They will not see a weapon, and the odds are that neither will someone who wishes to do you harm.

Think about this and understand how you weaponize this simple everyday item. You put a few fingers into the handle and swing it like crazy. Smash this up against the face or side of the head, and the assailant will know  it. Hit the person hard enough, and you might be able to drop them to the floor.

Survive The Coming Storm – Weaponize – When A Gun Isn't The Answer – By Ray Gano

Stainless Steel Coffee Mug - http://tinyurl.com/PZ-Stainless-Mug

The key is to have things in you work area that do not raise suspicion. Look around your area. Look in your desk. What can you weaponize?

Everyone has pens and letter openers in their desk or in their work area. Think tactical and weaponize these simple items, and you then have a tactical letter opener or tactical pen.

Tactical Letter Opener / Pen Set - http://tinyurl.com/PZ-Tactical-Letter-Opener

In fact, here is the pen, the tactical pen, that I carry all the time- the Uzi Tactical Pen. I have had my Uzi pen now for about 4 years. I love this pen, and it writes great. I like that I can get refills for it and it keeps writing.

Uzi Tactical Pen - http://tinyurl.com/PZ-Uzi-Tactical-Pen

Another weapon that you may not think about is scissors. But we are weaponizing ourselves and our environment.

Here is a great pair of scissors that will break apart and turn into two knives. Messermeister 8-Inch Take-Apart Kitchen Scissors. You can break these apart and put one in each hand. If you have been practicing the "heaven 6" duel stick form, then using these will be a breeze.

Messermeister 8-Inch Take-Apart Kitchen Scissors - http://tinyurl.com/PZ-Break-Apart-Scissors

If you do not know about the Heaven 6 form, here is my old teacher from Texas teaching Heaven 6 with knives - http://youtu.be/sr8nMpHRTSE

Here is my teacher giving a GREAT very easy knife drill that anyone can do in any shape or condition, this is a great technique especially for women - http://youtu.be/v2IMqjlEd_4

Every workplace has a stapler. This makes for a great impact weapon. Ever use a stapler to staple sheets of paper on the wall? You know how the open up so you can place the stapler end flat against a large flat surface? NOW... if you grabbed the stapler by the the "handle" side and allowed the "foot" to dangle free, you have a weapon that resembles an old fashioned

Sap. The common ol' stapler that most offices have is tough, sturdy and is built to take a beating. Just look at how often people slam it to staple a few pieces of paper. They have to be built tough. If your hand can wrap all the way around the stapler, you can use it as an impact weapon in an "ice pick" sort of method. Or you can wrap your  hand around it making a fist with it and punch a person with this, just like someone would hold a roll of dimes or brass knuckles.

Common Office Stapler - http://tinyurl.com/PZ-Stapler

Maybe having a steel knife is not allowed at the workplace. Then go with Cold Steel's Nightshade / FGX series of nylon knives.

Cold Steel Nightshade / FGX Boot Knife - http://tinyurl.com/PZ-Nightshade-knife

Cold Steel Nightshade / FGX Tanto - http://tinyurl.com/PZ-Nightshade-Tanto

Cold Steel Nightshade / FGX Tai Pan Dagger - http://tinyurl.com/PZ-Nightshade-Taipan-Dagger

The great thing about the CS Nightshade series is that they are a tough nylon that can stand up to a fight in an emergency. You can also take 440 / 800 grit sandpaper and literally put a close to razor's edge on these knives.

Because these are inexpensive, you can keep these nylon knives all over the work environment and even at home. Because they are impervious to the weather, you can keep them in your planter bed, in a fish tank, in the shower, in your car, or in your potted plant at work. You can hide these just about anywhere, and there is a perfect knife for every place you may want to hide one.

You can use one as a letter opener, or just keep one in each top drawer in your desk. Use the Nightshade / FGX spike in a potted plant. All the women usually have some teddy bear or stuffed animal in the office. Slice the top of the head and slip one of these knives inside the stuffed animal and set it on your desk.

Cold Steel Nightshade / FGX Skean Dhu -- http://tinyurl.com/PZ-Pocket-Dagger

These are very affordable so you can purchase 5-6 of these and hide them all over your office cubical as well as put them in strategic areas around your office that only you know. For example, get some Gorilla Duct Tape and tape one under the bathroom sink so that you know where it is, but it will not be easily found. Tape a Nightshade / FGX knife under the sitting area of your desk so that you have it right at the finger tips. All you have to do is drop your hands in your lap and reach up under the desk to pull it off.

Hiding the Cold Steel Nightshade / FGX Knife just about anywhere is possible. Then if the time arises that you need it, you have a weapon that is not rusted and is light and easy to use.

Gorilla Duct Tape - http://tinyurl.com/PZ-Gorilla-Duct-Tape

Start thinking about what you can wear that will not attract attention that you can weaponize.

Everywhere I go I wear my Infidel baseball cap. A baseball cap can be weaponized. I just discovered something called a Strike Spike. The Strike Spike is comprised of these wickedly sharp little discs that are meant to be threaded onto the strap of a baseball cap. If an enemy comes at you, it is natural instinct to raise your hands to protect your face. You can use this movement to then grab the bill of your baseball cap and then strike at the enemy with these Strike Spikes attached. These little babies turn your hat into a weapon. For $9.46 w/ Prime at Amazon, you can afford to outfit multiple hats with a set of these.

The Strike Spike - http://tinyurl.com/PZ-Strike-Spike

Ray's Infidel Baseball Cap - http://tinyurl.com/PZ-Infidel Cap

NOW, if you liked those Strike Spikes, then add fuel and

check out the GOTCHA cap. This is a baseball cap that has a built in weapon in the bill of the hat called the "HANOVER TOOLBOX" which is a Low Profile Less-Lethal Self-Defense Tool.

Here is how this weapon is described...

HANOVER TOOLBOX was created by a rare collaboration between three professional independent enterprises, all well-known leaders in their specific line of expertise; FAB-Defense® well experienced development team, product designer Dov Ganchrow and martial arts expert Yaron Hanover. The unique product line is designed to insure that you will never be caught empty handed. Advantages include the following: Made of reinforced durable polymer composite Easily carried - very compact State-of-the-Art ergonomic design Provides a simple and comfortable carry method Protection from the sun and much more Quick and easy to use Always within reach.

Gotcha Baseball Cap - http://tinyurl.com/PZ-Gotcha-Cap

I am also a huge fan of Cold Steel's Inferno Pepper Spray. This is not really a spray, but a foam that once it makes contact it melts. I like this compared to other sprays that can actually mist back into your face. Unless the wind is blowing, the Cold Steel Inferno will maintain its foam consistency till it hits the target. Folks this stuff is bad news to whom ever gets sprayed with it. They make it in all sorts of sizes, but for the office or work environment, they make a pen spray that slips into your shirt pocket. These are inexpensive and you can put one in your pocket, purse, keep a few in your desk at work, in your backpack, briefcase. You can keep these all over and never draw attention to what it is.

Cold Steel Pepper Spray Pen - http://tinyurl.com/PZ-Cold-Steel-Pepper-Pen

Something that I discovered a few years ago was the Self Defense Money Clip. I travel a lot and I have never had a problem getting these aboard an aircraft. These are great punching weapons that will do some serious damage. They are made from aircraft aluminum and you can put an edge on it so it will do more damage, but not so sharp that it will slice a hole in your pants. I have mine with me all the time, and it is easy to pull the bills off with your fingers while it is still in your pocket and then slip it over your middle finger.

Self Defense Money Clip - http://tinyurl.com/PZ-Self-Defense-Money-Clip

I highly recommend that people keep a good flashlight at their desk in case of an emergency. I have a couple that I recommend, and I own both.

First is the Zap Million Volt Flashlight. This is actually a rechargeable million volt stun gun and it is wicked. But you know what? It has a pretty good flashlight on it as well. This is perfect for the office, for on walks, keeping in your purse or backpack, use it to walk to  your car, there are a lot of uses for it. I have had mine for over 2 years and it still holds a great charge and push the button and it is like lightning going off. It is very easy to operate and even in a panic one could use it with ease.

The Zap Flashlight is also hefty enough that if you wanted to use it as an impact weapon, well it would do the job. It has some weight to it and it is a tad bulky. That is good when you need to slam this into someone and then let them have a million volts. You get this on any bad guy and push the button, they will drop. THEN.. while you have them down, I would zap them again for a good 10 seconds to make sure they are not getting back up for several long minutes. This is a good time to pull out the Cold Steel Pepper Spray and spray the bad guy in the face for a double whammy. They will not be getting up, and good chances are that you will be the hero of the office for taking out the bad guy.

Zap Million Volt Flashlight - http://tinyurl.com/PZ-Zap-Million-Volt-Flashlight

Now If you need serious light but also want to have some sort of impact weapon, then the Fenix PD35 is a great flashlight. I have one, and I also got one for Tracye. These run on CR123 lithium batteries so they last  a long time. I use mine almost daily and if I think that I will be out after dark, I clip it to my belt next to my cell phone holster.

This is a great light because it has multiple light settings, but set on the highest it shines around 900 lums. Point that in a bad guy's face, and it will blind them long enough for you to make a move and run or protect yourself.

Survive The Coming Storm – Weaponize – When A Gun Isn't The Answer – By Ray Gano

This light also as a strobe setting that is nice, but you need to be thinking ahead of time to be able to use it and time it properly. It is effective and it will blind a person as well as possibly confuse them for a second or two, again long enough to get away or draw one of your weapons to defend yourself.

Fenix PD35 960 Lumen CREE LED Tactical Flashlight - http://tinyurl.com/PZ-Fenix-Tactical-Flashlight

These are just a few ideas that can help you weaponize your workplace. But just because you have all these weapons around you, it will not help unless you practice situation awareness. You need to pay attention and grow eyes in the back of your head so that you have those few precious seconds to assess the situation, think out a quick plan and then weaponize yourself so that you can defend yourself and possibly protect those around you.

Escape and Evade Clothing – Getting Out of The Office

Survive The Coming Storm – Weaponize – When A Gun Isn't The Answer – By Ray Gano

In light of some of the events that have taken place where people are dealing with a lone terrorist / gunman, I wanted to give you some ideas on escape and evade clothing. Some of these items are made of  Kevlar, so will help protect you against cuts, scrapes, possibly even someone using a knife. Items like the Kevlar Sleeves are also heat resistant and are common in restaurants for people carrying and working with very hot plates, foods and dishes.

These items are NOT bullet proof, but if worn, it should help conceal your upper torso so that you can crawl, duck and take cover in an office / work environment and work to eventually make it to safety.

The Sap Hat I am including also doubles as a last ditch weapon. There are "BBs" sewn into the cap so that a person can use it as a bludgeoning weapon by grabbing the bill and swinging the cap.

Black Sap Hat - http://tinyurl.com/PZ-Sap-Hat

Survive The Coming Storm – Weaponize – When A Gun Isn't The Answer – By Ray Gano

Black Battle Scarf - http://tinyurl.com/PZ-Black-Battle-Scarf

Black Kevlar Sleeves - http://tinyurl.com/PZ-Black-Kevlar-Sleeves

Black Sports Mask - http://tinyurl.com/PZ-Black-Sports-Mask

Black Long Sleeve Kevlar Shirt - http://tinyurl.com/PZ-Black-Kevlar-Lsleeve-Shirt

Items I Recommended In This Chapter

Stainless Steel Coffee Mug - http://tinyurl.com/PZ-Stainless-Mug

Tactical Letter Opener / Pen Set - http://tinyurl.com/PZ-Tactical-Letter-Opener

Uzi Tactical Pen - http://tinyurl.com/PZ-Uzi-Tactical-Pen

Messermeister 8-Inch Take-Apart Kitchen Scissors - http://tinyurl.com/PZ-Break-Apart-Scissors

Common Office Stapler - http://tinyurl.com/PZ-Stapler

Cold Steel Nightshade / FGX Boot Knife - http://tinyurl.com/PZ-Nightshade-knife

Cold Steel Nightshade / FGX Tanto - http://tinyurl.com/PZ-Nightshade-Tanto

Cold Steel Nightshade / FGX Tai Pan Dagger - http://tinyurl.com/PZ-Nightshade-Taipan-Dagger

Cold Steel Nightshade / FGX Skean Dhu -- http://tinyurl.com/PZ-Pocket-Dagger

Gorilla Duct Tape - http://tinyurl.com/PZ-Gorilla-Duct-Tape

The Strike Spike - http://tinyurl.com/PZ-Strike-Spike

Ray's Infidel Baseball Cap - http://tinyurl.com/PZ-Infidel-Cap

Gotcha Baseball Cap - http://tinyurl.com/PZ-Gotcha-Cap

Cold Steel Pepper Spray Pen - http://tinyurl.com/PZ-Cold-Steel-Pepper-Pen

Self Defense Money Clip - http://tinyurl.com/PZ-Self-Defense-Money-Clip

Zap Million Volt Flashlight - http://tinyurl.com/PZ-Zap-Million-Volt-Flashlight

Fenix PD35 960 Lumen CREE LED Tactical Flashlight - http://tinyurl.com/PZ-Fenix-Tactical-Flashlight

Black Sap Hat - http://tinyurl.com/PZ-Sap-Hat

Black Battle Scarf - http://tinyurl.com/PZ-Black-Battle-Scarf

Black Kevlar Sleeves - http://tinyurl.com/PZ-Black-Kevlar-Sleeves

Black Sports Mask - http://tinyurl.com/PZ-Black-Sports-Mask

Black Long Sleeve Kevlar Shirt - http://tinyurl.com/PZ-Black-Kevlar-Lsleeve-Shirt

Survive The Coming Storm – Weaponize – When A Gun Isn't The Answer – By Ray Gano

CHAPTER 9 - Your Office Bug Out Bag / Get Home Bag

SO many of us think of bugging out of our home to get to a safe predetermined location.

But how many people have a bug out bag to get out of the work place?

Some people call this a "Get Home Bag."

This is a great bag to keep that "escape and evade clothing" that I talked about in the prior chapter. It is also wise to have other items like some food, water, meds, tools, and weapons.

Food & Water

If you have been a reader of mine, you know that I am a fan of the ER 3600 Calorie Bar. These bars taste great and are pre-scored into smaller bars that you can break off or easily cut off with a knife.

You can see the video here that I produced talking about the ER Bar.

WATCH NOW - https://youtu.be/fmzJwbTBGgs

Another item that you need to have in your Office Bug Out Bag / Get Home Bag is a means to contain and filter water.

I am a HUGE fan of Berkey water filters. We use them ourselves, and we even own a Royal Berkey Water Filter. These are the best water filters in the world. One of the best things you can put in your bag is a Berkey Sport bottle. This will filter 125 gallons of treated water or 75 gallons of swamp / muddy water. They are a great thing to have on hand to not only keep in your Office Bug Out Bag / Get Home Bag, but also to keep a few in the car and other places. You never know when you are going to need to get some water. They are inexpensive enough that you can purchase multiple bottles.

Here is a video of me when we lived in Texas drinking out of a skanky pool that our dogs and chickens used to drink out of and even bathe in.

WATCH NOW >> https://youtu.be/9_qmqfEwcEg

Finally, you want to have water in your bag just in case you cannot supply yourself before you leave your work area.

Emergency water pouches / boxes are a great way to go. The negative aspect is that they will weigh down your pack. Therefore, you need to really assess how much you will put in your pack to get you going until you can find some sort of water that you can use your Berkey Sport Bottle.

NOTE – if you have to seek out water, find your water source and make sure you hydrate yourself by drinking as much as you can at your water source. Then fill up your bottle on top of that.

Throw in a few salt packets or Gatorade packets in your bag so that you can put some in your mouth and then drink some water.

DO NOT ADD SALT OR GATORIAD TO THE SPORT BOTTLE. It will filter those things out as well. But you need replenish your electrolytes. So putting a little bit of powdered Gatorade in your mouth and then taking a swig of water will help you build those electrolytes back up again.

Another good thing is adding a bottle of salt pills. These will help you replenish your electrolytes as well. Keeping hydrated and the electrolytes up will help you in your trek home.

ER Emergency Ration 3600+ Calorie, 5-Year Emergency Food Bar - http://tinyurl.com/PZ-3500-ER-Bar

Berkey 22-Ounce Water Filter Sports Bottle - http://tinyurl.com/PZ-Berkey-Sport-Bottle

Emergency Water Packets – http://tinyurl.com/PZ-Emergency-Water

Electrolyte salt pills - http://tinyurl.com/PZ-Electrolyte-Salt-Pills

Gatorade packs - http://tinyurl.com/PZ-Gatorade-Packs

Gun Shot Kit / First Aid Kit

Another item that you want to have in your bug out bag is medical supplies like an Israeli Compression bandage, Tourniquet, or quick clot blood clotter. These are needed just in case one sustains gun shot or bad a knife cut. If there is a terror event taking place, there could be a chance that you could get cut or shot. You will need to have the items on hand to stop the bleeding.

Something else that a number of people have told me about is having a small tampon in your gun shot kit. A small tampon can be pushed into the bullet hole and then deployed into the wound. The small size tampon is about the size of a 9 mm to .45 caliber bullet. These are made to stop the bleeding and that is what you have to do. Having a few sanitary pads also is also good for knife wounds, bad cuts and scrapes. Again, these are made to hold blood and can help stop the bleeding. You can use some Gorilla Duct Tape to keep these things in place. I talk about that later on.

Another thing to have in your blow out kit is super glue. You would be amazed at the first aid uses super glue has. It is great at closing up a cut quickly. This is why I always keep it on hand.

Having a basic first aid kit in your bag is also a good idea. I created my own and have multiple zip lock bags already to go depending on what I need them for.

For example, I have a "blow out" kit. This is for gun and knife wounds, and I have all I need in that zip lock bag ready to go.

I then have my basic first aid zip lock bag with all I would need to treat basic wounds, sore muscles, burns, stings and other injuries.

My final bag is my own odd assortment of stomach meds, allergy meds, head ache, nausea, and whatever else I can think of.

But if you want to keep things simple, then I like the Coleman's Expedition First Aid Kit. It has 205-Pieces. It is slim in a neoprene sort of case. This will fit well in your middle or front compartment. What is nice is there is enough room to add to this kit some items that you want, for example, a "blow out" kit, some stomach meds, or something for sore muscles.

Israeli Compression Bandage - http://tinyurl.com/PZ-Israeli-Compression-Bandage

Military Issue Combat Application Tourniquet - http://tinyurl.com/PZ-Tourniquet

Quick Clot Blood Clotting Agent - http://tinyurl.com/PZ-Quick-Clot

Coleman First Aid Kit - http://tinyurl.com/PZ-Coleman-First-Aid-Kit

Just a Note on Sore Muscles

This is something that a lot of people do not think about to put in their bug out bags / Get Home Bag. You are probably going to have to walk home. That may be 10, 20, 30 plus miles. You will be sore. Muscles will hurt.

So it is a great idea to keep something for sore muscles such as pain relievers. Personally I LOVE tiger balm, and in fact, we use it all the time. It comes in a really  small jar that you can keep in the first aid kit. A little bit goes a long way.

Keeping a few pairs of extra socks and a few pairs of extra underwear also in your bag is a very good idea. You do not need clean pants or shirts, but clean socks and underwear are not only a pick me up motivator, but it will help prevent blisters, chafing and fungal infections. Putting a small bottle of Gold Bond Medicated Powder in your bag is also a good idea. This will help prevent any fungal infections taking root.

Believe me, I speak from experience. When I was in Spec Ops and out in the field, we easily walked 20 + miles a day with a heavy rucksack on our back. Having fresh socks, underwear and some body powder was like a blessing from heaven. If you have to walk home, you will be glad for the little comforts as well.

There is an old saying "Take care of your feet and they will take care of you." Believe me, this is gospel truth there friend.

Tiger Balm - http://tinyurl.com/PZ-Tiger-Balm

Gold Bond Medicated Powder - http://tinyurl.com/PZ-Goldbond-Powder

Clothing, Shoes, Hat & Gloves

While we are talking about extra socks and underwear, if you have to wear more "business attire" that is not made to withstand the elements, you may want to put a change of clothes in your bag as well as a good pair of hiking boots. You can tie the boots to the outside of your bag to save space.

A good pair of jeans and several shirts is a good idea. Think layers, starting with a "T-Shirt, " then a long sleeve shirt, and then even a long sleeve wool shirt or light jacket depending on where you are located. IF you are in a colder region, you may want to pack some Thermasilk long underwear. Yes, they are more expensive, but they keep you warmer. They are also lighter to carry instead of the bulky cotton ones you normally find.

It is always good to have some sort of head covering like a good baseball hat, stocking cap or both. You lose the most amount of your body heat from your head. IF you keep it covered, it helps keep in the heat. A hat also protects your head from the elements and will provide a bit of a cushion if you bump your head against some low hanging branch, or some sort of obstacle under which you may be crawling / ducking.

Finally, carry a good pair of gloves that allow your hands to breathe as well as protect your hands. I like the "Mechanic" brand of gloves. They are meant to take a beating, but they are thin enough to maintain your finger dexterity.

You want to wear gloves on this hike home. You may fall, need to climb walls or fences, crawl on the ground, or move debris. There are a number of things you may encounter where you may need to clear obstacles with your hands. Doing something like that  when your hands are not used to it, and without gloves, your hands are going to look pretty chewed up. You will need your hands to get you home, so make sure you protect them with a good pair of gloves that you can really work and maneuver in.

Thermasilk Pants - http://tinyurl.com/PZ-Thermasilk-Pants

Thermasilk Shirt - http://tinyurl.com/PZ-Thermasilk-Shirt

Mechanic Wear Gloves - http://tinyurl.com/PZ-Mechanics-Gloves

Tomahawk / Map & Compass

Other much needed tools to have in your Bug Out Bag / Get Home Bag are a tomahawk, map and compass. I personally recommend United Cutlery's M48 Ranger Hawk Axe with Compass. I personally have this very tomahawk, and I have put it through its paces. It is a GREAT cutter, and you can put a real good edge on it.

The compass is a good military type compass that paired with a map of your local area will help you get home.

I recommend having a tomahawk in your bag because it will double as a weapon or tool to cut open a door, break a window, chop wood or chop up a wooden pallet to make a fire.

The Tomahawk is a great all around tool and that is the reason many of the frontiersmen carried them.

The compass is needed to help you get home, especially if you have to go navigate areas you may not know or know as well. You do not know what sort of situation may be taking place, so you may have to avoid areas that have riots, fires, or other dangers. So having a map and compass in your Bug Out Bag / Get Home Bag is critical.

Tactical Tomahawk and Military Compass - http://tinyurl.com/PZ-Tomahawk-and-Compass

Poncho, Poncho Liner & Space Blanket

You have to think about how long it may take you to literally walk home. Many people commute and live far from where their home is located. So there is the possibility you might have to spend the night someplace.

Forget those "survival blankets" made out of mylar. They rip really easily. They are shiny like a mirror, and they are very noisy. Plus they really do not do a good job of keeping you warm. They cost what, $3.00 or so? Well you get what you pay for.

You need something that will help you get home that you can use multiple nights if is necessary.

When I was in Spec Ops, we did not have the luxury of sleeping bags. What we used was a wet weather poncho and a blanket type item called a poncho liner.

When you tie the poncho and liner together, you have a pretty good weather proof blanket that you can use to cover up and get a good night's sleep. The newer wet weather poncho also comes in a digital cammo pattern. Covering up with this item will also camouflage you and not draw attention to yourself. Being digital cammo, the pattern does well in both a city and urban and wooded environment. You need to remember that things may not be going well, and you will not want to draw attention to yourself. So remaining camouflaged may be something that you want to do and having a digital pattern poncho could help you with that.

NOW... to kick this up a notch, and this is what I personally carried, was an all-weather space blanket that is the same size as a military poncho. These blankets do not have the holes or hood cut outs in the middle. I tied my poncho liner into space blanket and had a great warm blanket. If you have a wife who likes

Survive The Coming Storm – Weaponize – When A Gun Isn't The Answer – By Ray Gano

to sew, have her sew the two together, but keep them seam on the edge so that there are no holes in the middle. That will prevent rain from seeping in. Just so you know, I have slept in mine in below 30 degree weather, and it kept me toasty warm.

How I used all these items together is explained below:

I would gather up a pile of leaves or pine needles. Once I had a good pile, I would cover that with my poncho. Then I lay on top of the soft pile covered with the poncho and then cover up with my space blanket and poncho liner. Let's just say that I started a trend with my team, and we all slept well... that is , when we were able to get some sleep.

A good military poncho and poncho liner will also help protect you from the elements, keeping you dry as well as warm as you are walking home.

Pairing the poncho with some 550 paracord, you can also make a shelter out of the poncho and still have the poncho liner to keep you warm.

Here are some examples...

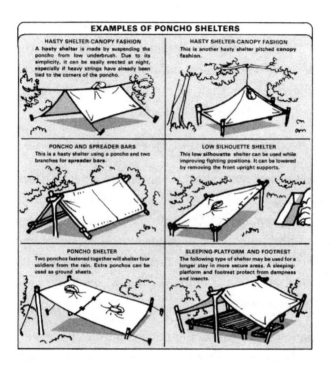

EXAMPLES OF PONCHO SHELTERS

HASTY SHELTER-CANOPY FASHION
A hasty shelter is made by suspending the poncho from low underbrush. Due to its simplicity, it can be easily erected at night, especially if heavy strings have already been tied to the corners of the poncho.

HASTY SHELTER-CANOPY FASHION
This is another hasty shelter pitched canopy fashion.

PONCHO AND SPREADER BARS
This is a hasty shelter using a poncho and two branches for spreader bars.

LOW SILHOUETTE SHELTER
This low silhouette shelter can be used while improving fighting positions. It can be lowered by removing the front upright supports.

PONCHO SHELTER
Two ponchos fastened together will shelter four soldiers from the rain. Extra ponchos can be used as ground sheets.

SLEEPING-PLATFORM AND FOOTREST
The following type of shelter may be used for a longer stay in more secure areas. A sleeping-platform and footrest protect from dampness and insects.

The military poncho is a very versatile tool. Couple that with a space blanket and poncho liner, and you are able to handle just about any inhospitable weather Mother Nature wants to throw at you. These items fold/roll-up pretty tight. They are light and easy to stuff in your small backpack Bug Out Bag / Get Home Bag.

Military Poncho Digital Cammo – http://tinyurl.com/PZ-Military-Poncho-Digitalcamo

Poncho Liner - http://tinyurl.com/PZ-Poncho-Liner

Survive The Coming Storm – Weaponize – When A Gun Isn't The Answer – By Ray Gano

All Weather Space Blanket - http://tinyurl.com/PZ-Space-Blanket

1000 Ft of Black 550 Paracord - http://tinyurl.com/PZ-Black-550-Paracord

Sturdy Computer Back Pack

So, what do you carry all this stuff in?

I personally have a Samsonite Tectonic Large Backpack. This backpack has been with me when I speak at conferences; it has traveled with me to Belize, Costa Rica and now here in Panama. I have literally abused this bag, but it just keeps going. As you can see in the picture, I always keep it somewhat packed and ready to go. All I need to do is slip my laptop, kindle, a few other items like my tomahawk / survival knife in it, and it is ready to go.

Some attractive features are that some of the more critical zippers are " self-healing," with also nice back comfort pads all in the right places. The back pads also have channels so that if you are wearing it for a long time, your back still gets some ventilation.

This is one tough bag, and I have worn out a few of my other back packs, but this one just keeps going. The quality is great, and none of the seams have given out or torn. This has easily weighed at times, over 50 lbs when I had it stuffed full with just about everything I need. The zippers did not pop, and the strap seams held up even when I am swinging it up on my back fully loaded.

ONE negative aspect is that there are so many zippered pockets that you will lose stuff in this backpack. Over the years I have learned to compartmentalize the back pack.

 Here is what I have done...

The first small pocket - at the very bottom, that holds my MP3 Player, clippers, chap stick and any meds that I need quickly.

The netted pocket - I do not put much in that I do not want to lose. So I mainly keep wet wipes in that so I can get to them in a hurry if I need them.

Samsonite Computer Backpack - http://tinyurl.com/PZ-Samsonite-Computer-Backpack

First Main Compartment

The first main zippered compartment is all my first aid gear, and I tend to carry a lot of that. Every time we have run into a situation and I did not have the proper meds, I adjust my med carry. As I mentioned before, I separate the first aid items out based on the use and keep them in heavy duty freezer zip lock bags. This way I can grab that certain bag, and it has everything I need.

This compartment also has two main pockets and a divider to keep pens, pencils, other small items. That is where I keep my note making items, a small folder knife and my Fenix Flashlight. There is a built in snap link cord that I hook to my flashlight so that I do not lose it. I also might hook my keys to that as well. The second pocket I will keep a battery backup power source to power up my cell phone or whatever may need charging. I also will keep my Kindle in this pocket for quick access.

Fenix PD35 960 Lumen CREE LED Tactical Flashlight - http://tinyurl.com/PZ-Fenix-Tactical-Flashlight

Second Main Zippered Compartment

This is where I keep all my electronic items, cameras, cables, extra batteries. I have other items like some

Survive The Coming Storm – Weaponize – When A Gun Isn't The Answer – By Ray Gano

extra clothes, my ER bars and empty water bottle. This area is also divided into two main compartments with pockets on the dividers. There is also a pocket on the front wall of the compartment. This is why I say that you can lose stuff in this backpack because of all the pockets. That front wall pocket I will keep more batteries and smaller items and my cell phone wall charger so that I know where it is. All I need to do is reach in, run my hand down that front wall, and it will go into that pocket. Then I can feel for my wall charger pretty quickly.

If you have not gathered it by now, this is my catch all pocket from food, clothes, electronic gear and whatever else I want to throw in here. This is the largest of the compartments. The second pocket in this main area is where I keep my tomahawk or my Blackhawk Tatang knife, or even both. There is enough room for that.

My Tatang Survival Knife

If you are looking for a great survival fixed blade knife, I HIGHLY recommend this knife. It is a high carbon steel knife that I can sharpen to a razor edge with a rock if I have to. This is why I love higher carbon based knives. This blade is so sharp I can literally shave with this knife.

Here is my Tatang in relation to a K-Bar. As you can see, this knife has got some heft. You are able to also choke up on the blade to give you more fighting agility. Hold it by the grip, and it will hack into any tree or lop of any branch you need it too. I have also sharpened the top edge, which was sharp when I pulled it out of the box, but now it is razor sharp. This knife with its "Spear point" can literally double if need be as a spear. Strap it on with some 550 cord to a long stick, and you have a pretty formidable weapon for defense. It can also be used to hunt if you have too.

It is also very versatile. You can dig with this knife, chop as I mentioned, and even use it to skin out a deer or hog. The edge holds pretty well, and I was really surprised. This is a knife that you could even throw if need arose. However, it would take some practice to do that.

Survive The Coming Storm – Weaponize – When A Gun Isn't The Answer – By Ray Gano

This is a beast of a knife. It is one of my top ten knives out of all the knives I own and definitely my "go to" knife if I needed to be in a survival situation. That is the main reason I purchased it.

Blackhawk Tatang Knife - http://tinyurl.com/PZ-Blackhawk-Tatang-Knife

Now back to the back pack...

Third Zippered Compartment

This is the one that is meant to hold your computer. I have an HP laptop, and it fits mine perfectly. I do not worry about it getting damaged or banged around. One drawback is that you may want to put a little padding at the bottom just to give it some extra cushion to protect your laptop. I am always looking out for my laptop because without it.... there goes my livelihood. So I may be a little over protective...therefore the little extra padding.

As this compartment is not that wide, it really is meant for your computer, mouse, power cord, and mouse pad. You can also put your iPad or Kindle in here as well with some spare room so that they are not plastered up next to each other.

Other Gear You May Want

I have other odds and ends gear that I like to keep in my bag, some of which you may be interested in having also.

A Survival Whistle – I can whistle pretty loud, but it is good to have a real survival whistle that can be heard from a good distance. It is best to get a marine survival whistle. This has a higher pitch and is meant to be heard over lower decibel sounds like waves, wind and splashing. People hear that high tone, and it just does not blend into the natural sounds.

Marine Survival Whistle - http://tinyurl.com/PZ-Marine-Survival-Whistle

Leatherman SkeleTool CX Multitool – This is a great multi tool, but it is on the expensive side because it is the one made with carbon fiber, which makes the weight about 5 ounces. This has all the basic tools that you really need which are the following:

- A lock blade Knife
- Screw driver with philips and flat head bits
- Needle Nose Pliers

- Regular and Hard Wire cutters
- Bottle Opener / Carabiner

Truly, those are all the tools that you will really need in the day to day life. I have used my Leatherman for a million and one things. I got it when they first came out, and I have loved it ever since. You can carry it on your belt loop, which is what I often do, or slip it into your pocket. There is a belt holster you can get for them, but I don't like those so I don't use it. Clipping it on my right side belt loop and then my cell phone can also help hold it in place which I do clip to my belt.

Here is a video review I did several years ago - https://youtu.be/_WbVycdnZbw

Leatherman Skeletool CX - http://tinyurl.com/PZ-Leatherman-Skeletool-CX

Uzi Tactical Pen – I know that I have talked about this already, but I LOVE my Uzi Tactical Pen. I have had my Uzi pen now for about 4 years. I love this pen, and it writes great. I like that I can get refills for it, and it keeps writing. I keep this in the pen area of the back pack.

Uzi Tactical Pen - http://tinyurl.com/PZ-Uzi-Tactical-Pen

Cold Steel Inferno Pepper Spray Pen – Alongside my Uzi Tac Pen is my Cold Steel Inferno Pen. This thing is great. You can carry it with you in your shirt pocket. It really looks like it is a fountain type pen. What I like about Cold Steel Inferno is that it is foam not a liquid spray. One of the problems with most pepper sprays is that if there is any wind or breeze, the liquid has a that some of the spray droplets / mist blowing back in your own face, thus defeating the purpose. Cold Steel's foam does not do that. The foam attaches itself to the face and then instantly melts from the heat of the skin. So wiping it off is difficult. When it liquefies, it will run into the eyes, mouth and easily be sucked into the nose. One good shot in the face with Inferno will dilate the capillaries of the eyes causing temporary blindness. It will induce choking, coughing and nausea and most importantly, trigger an immediate and massive sneeze reflex (due to the atomized black pepper particles) that will drag the super hot Habanero chili extract deep into the mucous membranes of the sinus cavities of the nose, throat and lungs. This reaction causes them to swell up and prevent all but desperate life support breathing.

Cold Steel Inferno Pepper Spray Pen - http://tinyurl.com/PZ-CS-Pen-Pepper-Spray

Spyderco Resilience G-10 Plain Edge Knife / Cold Steel Voyager Clip Point XL – This is one of my "EDC" knives. I like big folders, and I swap out between this and my Cold Steel Voyager Clip Point XL folder. Right now this is the one that I am carrying. I love it. What is great about the Spiderco knives is that you can do a red-neck fix on them by putting a zip tie on the ring. This procedure allows the blade to be deployed as you are pulling it out of your pocket.

This is a great all around carry knife that you can keep in your Office Bug Out Bag / Get Home Bag, or do what I do and swap out knives from time to time. So right now my Cold Steel Voyager XL is in my bag, but I will probably want to start carrying that again and put the Spiderco back in.

Both of these knives are big folders, or what some people call "pocket swords." What I like about these sorts of knives is that I am able to "flick" them open with some practice, thus speeding up the deployment. If you need your knife in a hurry, then this is a great move to learn how to do. Once you learn how to flick it open, it is a noise that people just know and raises the hair on the back of their necks.

Here is a video review that I did a while back on the Cold Steel Voyager Large and the XL knife.

WATCH NOW - https://youtu.be/7PPQurggMNk

Spiderco Resilience Lock Blade Knife - http://tinyurl.com/PZ-Spyderco-Resilience-Knife

Cold Steel Voyager XL Clip Point - http://tinyurl.com/PZ-CS-Voyager

Gorilla Duct Tape – Yep, every guy needs duct tape. It is what holds the world together. But I really love Gorilla Duct Tape. This stuff really sticks, and the cloth tape itself is heavy duty. Odds are that if you are a guy reading this, you have already worked with Gorilla Duct Tape and you love it as much as I do. Either you can keep the whole roll in your bag or do like what I do and roll up about 20 feet on your own. It is easy to do...just start unrolling it and roll it back up on itself. I used a wooden dowel to roll it back onto it self just to give it some rigidity. You can also fold back on itself and accomplish the same thing.

Gorilla Duct Tape - http://tinyurl.com/PZ-Gorilla-Duct-Tape

Items I Recommended In This Chapter

ER Emergency Ration 3600+ Calorie, 5-Year Emergency Food Bar - http://tinyurl.com/PZ-3500-ER-Bar

Berkey 22-Ounce Water Filter Sports Bottle - http://tinyurl.com/PZ-Berkey-Sport-Bottle

Emergency Water Packets – http://tinyurl.com/PZ-Emergency-Water

Electrolyte salt pills - http://tinyurl.com/PZ-Electrolyte-Salt-Pills

Gatorade packs - http://tinyurl.com/PZ-Gatorade-Packs

Tiger Balm - http://tinyurl.com/PZ-Tiger-Balm

Gold Bond Medicated Powder - http://tinyurl.com/PZ-Goldbond-Powder

Thermasilk Pants - http://tinyurl.com/PZ-Thermasilk-Pants

Thermasilk Shirt - http://tinyurl.com/PZ-Thermasilk-Shirt

Mechanic Wear Gloves - http://tinyurl.com/PZ-Mechanics-Gloves

Israeli Compression Bandage - http://tinyurl.com/PZ-Israeli-Compression-Bandage

Military Issue Combat Application Tourniquet - http://tinyurl.com/PZ-Tourniquet

Quick Clot Blood Clotting Agent - http://tinyurl.com/PZ-Quick-Clot

Super Glue Single Packs - http://tinyurl.com/PZ-Super-Glue-Single-Packs

Coleman First Aid Kit - http://tinyurl.com/PZ-Coleman-First-Aid-Kit

Tactical Tomahawk and Military Compass - http://tinyurl.com/PZ-Tomahawk-and-Compass

Military Poncho Digital Cammo – http://tinyurl.com/PZ-Military-Poncho-Digitalcamo

Poncho Liner - http://tinyurl.com/PZ-Poncho-Liner

All Weather Space Blanket - http://tinyurl.com/PZ-Space-Blanket

1000 Ft of Black 550 Paracord - http://tinyurl.com/PZ-Black-550-Paracord

Samsonite Computer Backpack - http://tinyurl.com/PZ-Samsonite-Computer-Backpack

Fenix PD35 960 Lumen CREE LED Tactical Flashlight - http://tinyurl.com/PZ-Fenix-Tactical-Flashlight

Blackhawk Tatang Knife - http://tinyurl.com/PZ-Blackhawk-Tatang-Knife

Marine Survival Whistle - http://tinyurl.com/PZ-Marine-Survival-Whistle

—

Leatherman Skeletool CX - http://tinyurl.com/PZ-Leatherman-Skeletool-CX

Uzi Tactical Pen - http://tinyurl.com/PZ-Uzi-Tactical-Pen

Cold Steel Inferno Pepper Spray Pen - http://tinyurl.com/PZ-CS-Pen-Pepper-Spray

Spiderco Resilience Lock Blade Knife - http://tinyurl.com/PZ-Spyderco-Resilience-Knife

Cold Steel Voyager XL Clip Point - http://tinyurl.com/PZ-CS-Voyager

Gorilla Duct Tape - http://tinyurl.com/PZ-Gorilla-Duct-Tape

CHAPTER 10 – Tools To Defend Your Vehicle - Carjacking

I left this section for last because I want to make a disclaimer here. In many states it is against the law to conceal weapons in your car. If you are caught, you could be arrested and jailed for having a concealed weapon. You need to check your state's laws and determine what you can and cannot carry.

In some states, like Texas for example, the "castle law" extends to your personal vehicle. So you are allowed to carry weapons to protect yourself while you remain in your car.

So you need to weigh the pros and cons of what you will and will not carry to defend yourself while you are driving in your car.

Carjacking – The Main Crime You May Face While In Your Vehicle

Police officers and security experts say that carjacking is preventable if one stays alert to their surroundings. In many cases good situational awareness will save your life at home, in the workplace, in the vehicle and in other public places.

Here are some things to be aware of to try to prevent a carjacking...

Before You Get To Your Car

- Be aware of your surroundings when entering and exiting your vehicle. Notice who is around you or if you are potentially being followed.

- Try to walk to your car with another person if possible, especially at night or in an unfamiliar area.

- Avoid parking near objects that someone can hide behind, such as dumpsters and large bushes.

- Trust your instincts! If an area feels unsafe, it probably   is.

- Avoid parking your vehicle in areas that aren't well lit.

Survive The Coming Storm – Weaponize – When A Gun Isn't The Answer – By Ray Gano

Once You Are In Your Car

- **Once in your Vehicle, keep your windows up and doors locked... ALWAYS**!

- When stopped for a traffic light or other reasons, carefully observe what is happening around your car via your side and rear view mirrors.

- Keep your purse, laptop and other valuables out of view while driving.

- Drive in the center lane to avoid being pushed over to the shoulder.

- Don't stop at isolated cash machines or other isolated areas.

- Don't stop to help a disabled motorist or pedestrian. Stay in your locked car and offer to call a service station or the police from your cell phone.

- Don't open your window for someone approaching your car asking for directions or trying to sell your something.

- Another ploy is someone with money saying that you dropped it. This is a popular thing to do at convenience stores and gas stations.

- Don't park your car in an isolated area.

- If you can't drive away from a bad situation, stay in your locked car and yell and honk your horn repeatedly. Criminals don't like noise, and they tend to run away to avoid attention.

Areas or situations where carjacking takes place most...

- When the victim is stopped at a traffic light.

- The carjacker pretends to be stranded.

- The carjacker fakes an accident to get you out of your car.

- The carjacker attacks the victim as they get in their car in parking garages, shopping mall and complex parking, and driveways.

Survive The Coming Storm – Weaponize – When A Gun Isn't The
Answer – By Ray Gano

- The best defense against a carjacking is having more than one person in the car.

- Always have your cell phone charged and a working charger in the car. Get in the habit to plug your phone into your charger when you get into your car.

Dealing With An Armed Carjacker

The armed carjacker is someone more and more people have to deal with. Today's world statistics show that an armed carjacker with a gun will most likely use it and try to kill you once they have taken you out of the car. You are literally being put in a life or death situation.

IF YOU DO NOTHING, MOST LIKELY YOU WILL BE KILLED. YOU MUST ACT & ACT QUICKLY!

So you need to do all you can as fast as you can to save your life.

Here is an excellent video on how to defend yourself against someone with a gun utilizing Krav Maga Techniques. For those who do not know, Krav Maga is an Israeli Martial Art specifically created for the Israeli army's Special Forces.

Carjacking Defense - Krav Maga Technique - w/ AJ Draven - https://youtu.be/V585rdvPDAA

Watch this over and over again and play it through your head often. When you pull up to a stop light, play the scenario through your head and practice the hand movements while waiting for the light to turn green.

What you are doing is mentally conditioning yourself and your sub conscious to react to an armed carjacker. By doing this training in your mind, your brain will go into action if you ever have to protect yourself in this life or death situation.

Just about any scenario that you will face in your vehicle can be correlated to a carjacking of some sort. So if you have all the bases covered to prevent a carjacking, you have covered many of the ways to protect yourself while in your vehicle.

The biggest lesson you need to take away is something we used to say in Ops all the time---- " Stay Alert – Stay

Survive The Coming Storm – Weaponize – When A Gun Isn't The Answer – By Ray Gano

Alive."

Weapons To Keep In Your Car

Again, you need to check the laws in your state. Many states come down pretty hard on people who keep concealed weapons in their cars.   Really do your homework.

I would recommend the following items:

Cold Steel Inferno Pepper Spray – This is a great go to weapon that you can keep in the middle console or in the coffee cup holder. There are a lot of places you can keep it where it is quickly assessable.

One warning though, and I speak from personal experience. If you live in a really hot climate, do not keep these items in your car. The summer heat will cause them to leak or explode. I used to keep the 1.3 ounce in my car while living in Texas. Well, I got in my car one day and heard a slight hissing sound. I looked in a little compartment that I kept my Cold Steel Inferno in and sure enough it was starting to leak. I quickly got it out of the car and then sprayed it into a weed bush. It gave me a chance to shoot it and see the foam in action. The stuff covered the weed bush I sprayed it at, and I got good coverage at 8 feet away. I had to use this pepper spray up right then and there, so I turned it into a learning lesson.

If you are going to use pepper spray, keep it in a somewhat cool environment and not in the Texas heat or very hot environment.

Cold Steel Inferno 2.5 oz / 70 grams - http://tinyurl.com/PZ-Cold-Steel-Inferno-70grams

Zap Million Volt Flashlight – I have talked about this stun gun in other chapters. I love this thing and in fact, I own other Zap products. I have been impressed with them, and my Zap flashlight is over 5 years old and still shocking big time. The key to using it as a car weapon is to be sure to keep it charged.

NOTE – Follow the instructions when it comes to charging your zap flashlight. They do not recommend charging it over 4 hours. I have been pretty religious about that, and mine works great. They also recommend that if you have not used it, to charge it every two months.

Zap Million Volt Flashlight - http://tinyurl.com/PZ-Zap-Million-Volt-Flashlight

Blackhawk Tatang Knife – Again I wrote about this in detail regarding my bug out bag / get home bag. This is a good knife to keep in the car as well. There are so many things you can use this knife for in a survival situation; so purchase a second one and keep it in your vehicle.

Blackhawk Tatang Knife - http://tinyurl.com/PZ-Blackhawk-Tatang-Knife

Cold Steel Kobun Tanto Knife – This is a great little boot knife, pretty flat and will fit nicely up under the visor of your car. I have one that I keep in my car, and it fits perfectly. I do not keep it in the scabbard. I have it positioned so that I can easily reach up there and by pulling the visor down, it falls naturally into my left hand in an "ice pick" grip. This way I can flip the visor down; the knife falls into my left hand, and I can instantly go into an ice picking motion, stabbing the assailant in the face, upper body, hands, or where ever the knife can make contact with his body.

This is a technique that you need to practice so that you have it in your mind. Also remember not to use your visor like you normally would. Having a sharp tanto knife dropping in your lap while driving would not be fun.

To train doing this and not get your hand all cut up, Cold Steel has the Kobun in their nightshade series. This is a nylon knife with a kraton handle, the same type that the real Kobun has so that you can get used to the grip.

Using this trainer, which can also double as a pretty effective weapon in and of itself, you can train dropping the knife into your left hand and then going into the "ice pick" motion. If you happen to grab the blade by mistake, you will not put a nasty cut into your hand.

Once you have trained with the Kobun trainer, you can then practice with the real blade by putting some duct tape over the blade. This way you get the feel and weight of the real blade dropping into your hand and then going into the "ice pick" motion.

An alternate idea is to rubber band the Kobun to the visor. This way if you forgot about the blade being there, it would still stay in place, and could still be accessible. The negative impact is that the rubber bands would defeat the ice pick technique spoken about earlier.

The key is really training at this technique. So you may wish to keep your Kobun trainer in the car with you and do some quick training while waiting in your vehicle or at a long stop light.

Cold Steel Inferno 2.5 oz / 70 grams - http://tinyurl.com/PZ-Cold-Steel-Inferno-70grams

Cold Steel Inferno 1.3 oz / 37 grams - http://tinyurl.com/PZ-Cold-Steel-Inferno-37grams

Zap Million Volt Flashlight - http://tinyurl.com/PZ-Zap-Million-Volt-Flashlight

Blackhawk Tatang Knife - http://tinyurl.com/PZ-Blackhawk-Tatang-Knife

Cold Steel Kobun Tanto Knife - http://tinyurl.com/PZ-CS-Kobun-Knife

Cold Steel Kobun Trainer - http://tinyurl.com/PZ-CS-Kobun-Trainer

Always Keep A First Aid Kit / Blow Out Kit in Your Car

In case you are assaulted, it is good to have the means to administer first aid to yourself or a passenger. Having a blowout kit (a kit specifically for gun and knife wounds) is also a very good idea.

Here is a little personal story about the importance of having a blowout kit in your car.

One day Tracye and I were at the park. I had a brand new knife that I was working with, learning how to deploy it and close it up with one hand. Well, in the process of practicing, I closed the knife on my right index finger and sliced it pretty bad. Fortunately, I had a first aid / blow out kit in the car, and I was able to administer first aid to myself and stop the bleeding. Remembering past lessons, I also keep multiple bottles of super glue in my blow out kit as well. These are great and have come in handy many times. If you like to collect and work with knives, you will eventually get cut. Super glue is basically what the hospitals use to close up cuts like this.

I was able to stop the bleeding, and yes it was spurting out; but I applied compression long enough to stop it and apply the super glue. I wrapped it up and in 24 hours the cut started to mend itself.

If I did not have a first aid / blow out kit in my car, I would have bled all over the place and would not have been able to stop the bleeding.

These are items I recommend keeping in your vehicle at all times...

Israeli Compression Bandage - http://tinyurl.com/PZ-Israeli-Compression-Bandage

Military Issue Combat Application Tourniquet - http://tinyurl.com/PZ-Tourniquet

Quick Clot Blood Clotting Agent - http://tinyurl.com/PZ-Quick-Clot

Super Glue Single Packs - http://tinyurl.com/PZ-Super-Glue-Single-Packs

Coleman First Aid Kit - http://tinyurl.com/PZ-Coleman-First-Aid-Kit

Part 5

Training To

Defend

CHAPTER 11 - A Time To Train - Solo Training At Home - Recommended Videos

Recently news came out that Abu Bakr al-Baghdadi, leader of the ISIS revolution, swore a vow to kill all infidels, non-Muslims.

I got an email from a PZ Insider down in Australia. He told me that there are already reported 100+ Australian Muslims who have gone to fight for ISIS. Most of these people are Aussie Converts to Islam.

In the US Islam is gaining converts daily, probably by the hundreds if not more. When you look at our youth today who have no moral grounding and looking for "purpose," Islam has a strong pull and attraction to our youth today.

Mosques are turning up all over in the US.

Survive The Coming Storm – Weaponize – When A Gun Isn't The Answer – By Ray Gano

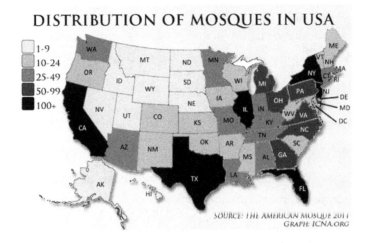

DISTRIBUTION OF MOSQUES IN USA

SOURCE: THE AMERICAN MOSQUE 2011
GRAPH: ICNA.ORG

The above map is from 2011. I know these numbers have grown if not doubled and even tripled in some areas.

I think you can see the picture that I am painting here.

We need to be ready to defend and fight even without guns. We may even have to be in a position that we have our guns "cached" somewhere to be pulled out for another day.

If that is the case, what do we do to protect ourselves and fight if we are put in that situation?

This is why I promote learning alternate weapons like the sword, knife, fighting sticks, and other items.

Survive The Coming Storm – Weaponize – When A Gun Isn't The Answer – By Ray Gano

Not only do I promote it, but I am now of the mindset that we need to be actively training and learning... NOW.

I see Jihad coming to our shores.

How can I say that?

We were once a God fearing country. We are that no longer. We export our filth, sin, homosexual activity, hedonism, abortion, and every other vile thing our nation produces to the world. We now revel in our sin. We spit in God's face.

I believe that God has been warning our nation for some time now that HIS Chastisement is coming.

I cover this in my book in detail - "Israel - America & God's Judgment" You can order it from Amazon for the KINDLE

In my book I talk about how God Judges the Nations. The template to that is found in Isaiah 5.

The first part of Isaiah 5 talks about the sins in which our nation participates.

BUT.. it is in the last part of Isaiah 5 that we read how God chastises the nation.

Musashi
High Carbon Steel
Iaito Katana
(unsharpened)

He ALWAYS uses the enemies of the nation that have backslidden against Him.

We read in Isaiah 5:26-30 ...

> 26 And he will lift up an ensign to the nations from far,
> and will hiss unto them from the end of the earth:
> and, behold, they shall come with speed swiftly:
> 27 none shall be weary nor stumble among them;
> none shall slumber nor sleep;
> neither shall the girdle of their loins be loosed,
> nor the latchet of their shoes be broken:
> 28 whose arrows are sharp, and all their bows bent,
> their horses' hoofs shall be counted like flint,
> and their wheels like a whirlwind:
> 29 their roaring shall be like a lion,
> they shall roar like young lions:
> yea, they shall roar, and lay hold of the prey,

and shall carry it away safe, and none shall deliver it.

30 And in that day they shall roar against them like the roaring of the sea:

and if one look unto the land, behold darkness and sorrow,

and the light is darkened in the heavens thereof.

Whenever I read the above Scripture, I am reminded of Muslim hordes rolling over our nation, much like ISIS rolled over Syria and Iraq. They moved just like a plague of locust destroying everything in their wake.

Musashi - 1060 Carbon Steel Differentially Hardened Katana (battle ready sword)

With all this said, I believe that it would behoove us all to start training with weapons.

Christ himself said ...

Luke 22:36 Then said he unto them, But now, he that hath a purse, let him take it, and likewise his scrip: and he that hath no sword, let him sell his garment, and buy one.

MEN - HUSBANDS - FATHERS -- We are to ensure the health and welfare of our families. We are to give our lives if need be to protect our loved ones.

True warriors fight not because they hate what is in front of them. They fight because they love what is behind them.

Scripture says...

1 Timothy 5:8 But if any provide not for his own, and specially for those of his own house, he hath denied the faith, and is worse than an infidel.

Foam Padded
Fighting Stick
(26-Inch)
buy two of these
you will need them

That "provide" spoken in Timothy means in all areas... health, welfare, food, clothing, and security.

I have put together a series of videos based on the weapons as well as teachers that I have taken lessons from.

My criteria for teachers and training methods are the following:

1 - I can train from home.

2 - I am getting up there in age, so my body has to be able to hang with it.

3 - I do not need a training partner or a special place. Living room, garage, back yard, or other areas is where I train.

4 - I am able to gasp the ideas and then teach others how to fight as well.

5 - I do not care about black belts and the purist forms. All I care about is taking my enemy out with extreme bias, then walking away from the fight, and living to tell about it another day.

Much of my focus centers on Filipino fighting sticks. I have been involved with fighting sticks for several years now. I took lessons in person when I lived in Texas and now on the internet.

The methodology that I am learning is called "K4S" or Knife for Street. My teacher goes by the handle "Wmpyr." He is one of the best solo trainers out there on the internet today.

His ultimate goal when teaching is that you can pick up any item and use it as a weapon if you learn a few basic techniques. The first technique he teaches is called the "Heaven 6." He has adapted this method to fit more of a "street mode" vs a purist mode.

He also focuses on solo training or training by yourself and in the privacy of your own home. All the things he teaches does not require a training partner or to be in a special setting. If you have space in your living room, back yard, bedroom, any other personal space…. you can train.

This is one of the benefits that attracted me to his methodology when I lived in Texas, and I still watch his lessons and learn more and more from him and his training.

My second teacher is one who focuses on the Samurai

Survive The Comi

Cold Steel Training Katana

sword, Dana Abbott. The sword style that Dana teaches is called Iai-batto-do. This style is Japanese military sword fighting. It is a system that is easy to teach, easy to learn and that was what was needed for the Samurai and Japanese military. They had to teach their soldiers how to quickly fight and to use the sword. Dana says "The katana only takes minutes to learn, but a life time to perfect." It is true; one can learn to use the sword pretty quickly.

Dana also focuses on solo training because this is the way of the Samurai. So training in your back yard, garage or living room is also achievable following Dana's teaching.

Dana's / Iai-batto-do methodology consists of the following...

- 8 Stances
- 8 Cuts
- 8 Draws
- 8 Sheaths
- 8 Forms / katas

Learn these, and you got the basics down.

Finally I want to share with you FORZA. It is an aerobic exercise that deals with a "Bokken" or wooden samurai sword. It is a great way to get in shape and is something that you can do in the privacy of your own home. It is a lot of fun, and you work up a pretty good sweat doing FORZA. At the bottom of the list I have linked in a

Dana Abbott's
Beginner's Guide
to Japanese Sword
Volume 1

FORZA playlist. I have not watched all these myself, but it will give you the idea. I watch several DVDs from Ilaria Montagnani who is the founder of FORZA to train with.

I will be creating a special PZ INSIDER ONLY page on the website that will have these as well as many other training links that I will be adding.

I am currently also learning Nunchucku (nunchucks), Sai, and a few other weapons. I will be sharing these training videos as well on that PZ Insider Only page that I will be building in the near future.

INTRO TO SOLO TRAINING - VIDEO TRAINING AT HOME - HAND HELD WEAPONS

STICK & IMPROVISED WEAPONS & HEAVEN 6 TECHNIQUE

Karambit, Pen, Machete, Flashlight, Heaven 6 -- http://youtu.be/8SNvwcFvVag

Intro to the Heaven 6 Technique Part 1 -- http://youtu.be/UwstZTy6lrQ

Intro to the Heaven 6 Technique Part 2 -- http://youtu.be/khecMEXO-j8

STICK FIGHTING heaven 6 generator for Ray -- http://youtu.be/r7j5EdG0Ea4

How to use the heaven 6 for self defense -- http://youtu.be/ijd5iZfkjA0

What is next after the heaven 6? --
http://youtu.be/KDLz-BQnBlw

KNIFE

Knife Heaven 6 -- http://youtu.be/sr8nMpHRTSE

Solo training 5 move basic knife drill --
http://youtu.be/v2IMqjlEd_4

Knife body mechanics figure 8 --
http://youtu.be/TkxzfzHxcQA

12 basic strikes using the knife stick fighting --
http://youtu.be/ETVs3FAV0sl

Espada y daga basic lesson (Stick & Knife) --
http://youtu.be/ZkkVURdmHV8

TOMAHAWK

Basic tomahawk exercises and techniques Pt 1 --
http://youtu.be/QuaFWM1Vdr0

Basic tomahawk exercises and techniques Pt 2 --
http://youtu.be/NwQnrx9P9p4

KATANA -- SAMAURI SWORD BASIC STRIKES

Kihon Workout Summary Part 1 --
http://youtu.be/7FL757tGWx8

Kihon Workout Summary Part 2 --
http://youtu.be/DPQ0tWV4LVk

Kihon Workout Summary Part 3 --
http://youtu.be/Phu0zFPubJU

Kihon Workout Summary Part 4 --
http://youtu.be/RTvTydhqm4o

Kihon Workout Summary Part 5 --
http://youtu.be/rJOie3bl0aM

KATANA -- DRAW, CUT, SHEATH CONCEPTS

Draw and Sheath Concepts Supplement 1 -
http://youtu.be/cwya8ynRj-0

Draw, Cut and Sheath Concepts Supplement 2 --
http://youtu.be/ppv_xn-x4lc

Drawing the Sword Concepts Supplement 3 --
http://youtu.be/LHo8B6WfT8Y

Reverse Draw and Thrust Concepts Supplement 4 --
http://youtu.be/iolYZ1DcGco

KATANA -- BACK YARD CUTTING

Practicing the Sword in Your Backyard: One --
http://youtu.be/qCXEgOm5ubU

Practicing the Sword in Your Backyard: Two --
http://youtu.be/ogbOmeUEGnM

Practicing the Sword in Your Backyard: Three --
http://youtu.be/JSMyXnL4r8w

SWORD WORKOUTS

1,234 Shinken Cuts (Spring Workout) --
http://youtu.be/X26lUmX6BZ0

Thanksgiving 1000 Calorie Cutter Workout --
http://youtu.be/3Xy1d39V3Gw

FORZA -- KATANA AROBIC WORKOUT PLAY LIST

http://www.youtube.com/playlist?list=PLpTMUIQwHi9
VszuCZ21GH8MAzCl6pdbAp

Survive The Coming Storm – Weaponize – When A Gun Isn't The
Answer – By Ray Gano

**Forza
The Samurai Sword
Workout DVD 1**

**Forza
The Samurai Sword
Workout DVD 2**

**Forza
The Samurai Sword
Workout Book**

**Dana Abbott's
Beginner's Guide to
Japanese Sword
Volume 2**

Survive The Coming Storm – Weaponize – When A Gun Isn't The
Answer – By Ray Gano

RAY'S BOOKS

Survive The Coming Storm – The Value of A Preparedness Lifestyle - http://tinyurl.com/STCS-Kindle-version

Survive The Coming Storm - Ebola Crisis: A Prepper's Guide on How To Prepare For A Killer Global Ebola Pandemic and Treat At Home - http://amzn.com/B00MI8LIXK

Survive The Coming Storm - The Poor man's Guide To Preserving Your Wealth In an Economic Collapse - http://amzn.com/B00WLLHKCW

Israel - America And God's Judgment - Discovering God's Biblical Template For Judging Nations http://amzn.com/B00GZ49ADS

Past The Point of No Return - Why 2 Chronicles 7:14 No Longer Applies To US ...At Least For Now By Ray Gano http://amzn.com/B00ANDCOYO

My Name Is Lucifer - Different Sects, Different Religions and Mother of All Harlots - http://amzn.com/B00IBLJQOG

SURVIVAL FOOD

If you are looking for Survival Food, check out Ray & Tracye Thrive Life Site http://www.thrivelife.com/Gano

MY SOCIAL MEDIA PAGES

Visit the Prophezine website (Main Site) at http://raygano.com

My personal page --
https://www.facebook.com/RayGano

The Servant Warrior FB Page --
https://www.facebook.com/groups/theservantwarrior/

The Prophezine FB Page --
https://www.facebook.com/groups/prophezine/

If you are on Twitter - please follow me at -
https://twitter.com/RayG_Prophezine

About The Author

Ray Gano and his wife Tracye live in the great state of Texas. They spent 4 years living in Central America, which was the impetus in writing this book. In Central America it is very difficult to own a gun. Ray start training with knife, stick and the deadly combative art "Wing Chun." Wing Chun is a devastating close quarter combat system. It is Ray's goal to eventually open a specialized school teaching realistic self-defense for a realistic world.

You can contact Ray at – ray.gano@raygano.com

CPSIA information can be obtained
at www.ICGtesting.com
Printed in the USA
LVHW081357180820
663514LV00018B/1659